INSTANT EXPERIENCE for REAL ESTATE AGENTS

**Great Lessons,
True Stories
and Lots of Fun
for Real Estate Agents**

by
David A. Thyfault

Printed in the United States of America by Lightning Source, Inc.

ISBN 978-1-937862-62-6

Library of Congress Control Number 2013953742

Cover design by Nathan Fisher.

This book available in digital format.

Published 2013 by BookCrafters, Parker, Colorado.
SAN-859-6352, BookCrafters@comcast.net

Copies of this book may be ordered from www.bookcrafters.net
and other online bookstores.

BookCrafters

DEDICATION

To Adam, Justin and Patty, the second-best
core family anywhere (the law of averages says there
must be a better one somewhere).
Each of you has blessed my life in ways
too numerous to count.
Thank you. Thank you. Thank you.

ACKNOWLEDGEMENTS

Inspiration and assistance for this book have come from all sorts of fine people. I have chosen not to include their last names to stay consistent with the material within the book, but they know who they are. My heartfelt thanks to all of you.

Contributions:

Natalie, John, Heather, Dan, Matt, Gretchen, Jerome, Adam, Becca, Ivan, Tanya, Peter, Jim, Kevin, Kathy, Justin, Donna, Sylvia, Ken, Elliot, Sean, Jeanine, Bob, Annie, Keith, Ryan, Chris, Duane, Margie, Larry, Jennifer, Rocky, Patty, Eric, Jace and Mark.

Inspirations:

Howard, Tom, Robin, Rickie, Steve, Ed, Stan, Gale, Billy, Scott, Mark, Al, Clark, Emily,

Louie, Rick, Chuck, Michael, Albert, Shirley, Cherlyn, Janet, Carol, Sarah, Hank and Mike.

All the folks who ever got a real estate license, whether things worked out for them or not

My own clients, customers, tenants and friends in the related businesses

The entire gang at Remax Professionals

The Association of Realtors

TABLE OF CONTENTS

INGRESS

Only two percent of those who pass the state exam for a real estate license are still in the business and working full-time after three years. I heard that startling statistic a couple of decades ago, and the basic dynamic remains: The fatality rate of new licensees is very, very (not over-stated) high. If that information is tempting you to put this book down right now and try something else that would be a mistake because there is some very good news for you. Please read on.

The above information would imply that the agents who do well in this business are extraordinary in some way, but that is simply not the case. This writer has known hundreds of them personally, and I assure you, they are very ordinary people, probably a lot like you.

So, all that sets up an interesting enigma: If most of the successful agents are common, ordinary people, why do so many equally promising new licensees fade away within a few months of getting their first box of business cards? The information in this book will answer that question and a whole lot more. The differences between the two groups are subtle but very powerful.

We are not going to discuss familiar topics like how to work expired listings or make effective listing presentations. There are already plenty of sources for that information. Instead, we are going to explore fresh new topics which licensees need to know in order to survive and succeed. You will uncover information the real estate schools do not tell you. You will also find out important facts your managing broker and other instructors do not usually discuss with you.

Until now, the information provided in this book has been very elusive to the new licensee because nobody had an incentive to assemble the information and share it with you. That is where I come in. Over a long and storied career, I came to understand what it really takes to succeed as a broker. I had to learn my information in the proverbial School of Hard Knocks. Most successful agents learned their lessons that same way. Fortunately, you don't have to plow that same old tired ground. A few hours with this book should help you join the "Two Percent Club."

I hope you will relate to me like a favorite uncle who is talking with you in your living room rather than as a stuffy-shirted professor, lecturing in a classroom. I will refer to myself as "Uncle Dave" but it would be weird to speak in third person all the time, so I do not do that. This less formal approach is intended as a constant reminder that I am a common guy, who learned his lessons in the streets, homes and offices of real live people, not from the theories of intellectuals.

I will consider this book a glowing success if either one of two contrary activities occurs. One is, you absorb this material, broaden your knowledge and enter the business better prepared to succeed and make worthy contributions. The other possibility is you discover you are not sufficiently prepared for this business at this time. If that happens, you win anyway. It is much better to find out what you need to know by spending a few hours with this book than it is to invest thousands of dollars and months of frustration to arrive at the same inevitable conclusion.

If the information you uncover causes you to have doubts about entering the sales side of the business, do not give up without reviewing the chapter subtitled "Jobs of the Industry." There are many career options in this business and I am certain there is something else for you. There are several other licensed positions including some with salaries and some that allow you to phase into the profession gradually. There are also plenty of clerical and support jobs available, both in the real estate offices and in the related professions.

Occasionally I will mention tax matters, marketing ideas, legal issues or some topics which may be unfamiliar to you. Naturally, I cannot know every situation in every market for every person before it comes up. Therefore, it is incumbent on you to do your own independent homework before you act on the ideas contained herein.

The words "agent," "licensee" and "broker" are used interchangeably throughout these pages. I fully realize that some states have a step-up process wherein a new licensee must be an "agent" for an apprenticeship period before he or she is eligible for a broker's license, but that distinction is not necessary here.

As you peel back the pages you will meet some of my friends and colleagues by first name. These are real people. Unless otherwise indicated their real names are usually used (with their permission).

Finally, for a change of pace, I have included a section called "Uncle Dave's True Story" at the end of each chapter. I was involved in all of these situations, sometimes as a broker, sometimes as a principal (the buyer or seller). While most real estate transactions fit a predictable and priceless pattern, occasionally we become embroiled in unusual circumstances which lend us extraordinary opportunities to learn something additional. These transactions are in the latter group. Most of the stories tie in especially well to the topics of the chapters that they follow but a couple of them are just good stories that lend worthwhile knowledge on their own.

You will gain the most "experience" if you imagine you were in Uncle Dave's shoes when these transactions unfolded and try to determine what lesson you could have absorbed from that experience. Just in case you miss the lessons, I have included them in the last chapter of this book, titled "Your Instant Experience."

Now that you understand the purpose of this book, it is time to find out just exactly who I am. Let me assure you, you are in for a surprise or two.

ABOUT UNCLE DAVE

Ordinarily, a biography is written in the third person, but Uncle Dave's background includes some less becoming experiences so this section does not lend itself to that style. Therefore, here is what you should know about me.

Prior to working fifteen years in one of the most dynamic RE/MAX offices anywhere, Uncle Dave spent seven years in four different entry-level type offices. I have worked with hundreds of beginners and hundreds of successful brokers. Along the way, I began a call-in radio program titled "Let's Talk Real Estate." Callers were invited to ask questions about their real estate matters. I also wrote some articles for a local newspaper and taught classes at a community college and local real estate offices. I have accumulated nearly 300 rental properties, including a couple dozen houses and condos, but mostly apartments.

I sold more than 600 homes before retiring. My highest-high was the month I earned $86,917.50 in commissions and my lowest-low was the time I suffered through five months with no income. After 22 years working full-time in the business, I earned over two million dollars in commissions.

Although there were plenty of other agents who sold more homes than I did, I had a secret weapon which enabled me to become the first person to retire out of that fantastic RE/MAX office, while I was still in my forties: I always believed I should be my own best client. By employing that concept, I earned another eight million dollars along the way. That combined effort of earning commissions plus profits from investments brought my average income to around a half-million dollars per year, weighted more heavily in the later years.

If you find yourself impressed, in any way, by my accomplishments you might suppose that success came easily to me, but the opposite is true. When it comes to successful real estate agents, very few of them have had so many hard lessons to learn. When you discover the rest of my story you might even consider it a miracle that one person could make so many stupid mistakes and still turn things around. Here is a little juicy background information for you:

I was surrounded by six sisters and raised in a lower-middle class neighborhood in West Denver. Although my parents were honorable people, there was so much activity in our large and hectic family that there was not much time for individual attention. Therefore, when it came to learning the important lessons of life, I was essentially left to my own devices. Naturally, when a lad is exposed to such unbridled freedom, he is bound to succumb to the whims of youthful indiscretions; hence, I made plenty of poor choices before I straightened out and eventually fulfilled my destiny.

I was basically a C student who could have done much better if I had had any interest in what they were teaching. In spite of that sub-par performance, I was the first person in our family to give college a try. That decision changed the course of my life. I found out right away that I wanted to get into the real estate business, but ironically, I did not learn that fact in a classroom.

The fathers of two of my classmates each accumulated a small portfolio of rental properties separate from their primary jobs. When I learned how those gentlemen turned ones into twos, I knew that was for me. It would take ten more years before I would obtain my real estate license. In the meantime, I still had a lot of mistakes to make and some more growing up to do.

For starters, I was introduced to marijuana that first year of college. I was like many others of the time and lent drugs too much importance, so I rarely went to class. Naturally, I flunked out. The next year I flunked out of a junior college, primarily for the same reason.

By the time I was nineteen, my friends and I were getting high fairly often. Whoever could find a supply of pot would buy a medium-sized quantity and recoup his money by distributing it among our small group and each recipient would pitch in his fair share of the cost. None of us were "dealers" in any sense of the word, but there was some selling and buying in those seemingly innocent exchanges between friends. Eventually a friend of a friend joined the group and I had the misfortune of "sharing" some pot with him in exchange for the $10 which I paid for it. As you probably guessed, he turned out to be an under-cover narcotics officer. I was arrested and convicted of a felony for selling $10 worth of marijuana (drug penalties in small towns were very harsh in those days). I went to jail for sixty days, beginning on my 20th birthday. That was where I started to realize that I needed to rethink my priorities. But, unfortunately, I still needed some more convincing.

Having no better ideas, I decided to work in the grocery business at Safeway. I did not want to start out with any strikes against me so I lied on my application about having been arrested. That worked out well and I got a job in the produce department. I applied myself and did fairly well. The next year I transferred to a different company and lied on my application again.

A little over a year later I made one of my few smart choices of those days; I married Patty, who would become my life partner.

I was beginning to think about real estate again and I invested in some land. Then I decided to get my license. The application for a license asked the same question I had seen on previous ones. Since lying about the arrest had worked before, I did it again. This time the outcome was different. The local Real Estate Commission did a background check and discovered the felony conviction of three years earlier. Obviously, they cannot approve people for real estate licenses if they know them to be liars, so they denied my license. That was very humbling and I decided it was time to stop hiding from my past. My newly established commitment was immediately tested.

The resident manager in our apartment building bought a home and that created an opening for the position. I called the professional manager and asked for an appointment to discuss the job. I poured out the whole truth about my past and he must have admired the candor because he decided to give us a chance. Finally, things were starting to look up.

A couple years later we moved to California and I decided to try for a real estate license in that state. This time I knew what to do. I told the whole truth and got references from the former property manager and my employers. I wrote a letter and explained what I had learned from all my mistakes. They issued a red probationary license which was unusual because all the other real estate licenses were either white or yellow. When my red license was hung by the others in the office, I had a lot of explaining to do. Nobody knew better than I did: Honesty was the best policy.

A little over a year passed and we decided it was time to put down roots and start our family. We elected to return to Colorado for that purpose. I worked in the grocery business for a while then I got my license and took a position working in a two-man sales department of the same property manager I mentioned earlier.

In those days, there was no Internet, and very few books or seminars on any phase of real estate sales or investing. Absent any traditional guidance, I continued to sell real estate and accumulate small rental properties any way I could.

After seven years I joined a very dynamic company, RE/MAX Professionals, in nearby Lakewood, Colorado. Unfortunately, more problems were just around the corner. In the mid-eighties, home prices in our community took a deep nose dive and we watched an impressive real estate portfolio fade away. Bankruptcy was inevitable. As you can imagine it would have been easy to quit at that time, but as you know by now, Uncle Dave is no quitter. Instead, I dusted myself off and started over, once again determined to learn from my mistakes. I formed a new investment philosophy which proved to be the solution to my financial problems.

Eventually, the market rebounded and new commissions were earned. In addition, the rental properties were generating real spendable cash flow and I finally understood the big picture. The next 13 years I employed the wisdom gained from my hard-learned lessons, both as a broker and an investor, and accomplished the important tasks mentioned earlier.

Now, I am essentially retired but I still love the real estate industry and I am in a position to "give back." I have trained others, written this book (with additional ones in the works) and I teach classes on the subjects of this book. As you might guess, somebody who has traveled so many unusual roads has plenty of interesting stories to tell.

I like to think my story is useful because it proves that if a lower-middle class, C student, double drop-out, bankrupt prisoner with six sisters and a red real estate license can overcome so many stupid obstacles, practically anybody else can succeed... and I would love to help you do just that!!!

So, let's get to it. Pull up a chair, grab a highlighter or two and let Uncle Dave share the insider's secrets of the real estate profession with you.

Chapter 1 – THE THREE-LEGGED STOOL OF KNOWLEDGE
or
Gathering Wisdom

If I were you, I would be wondering why I should read this book. What makes it different? Is it worth my time? Please let Uncle Dave assure you, you are starting off on the right foot. Those are very good questions. The answers to them, and a whole lot more, can be found in a symbolic piece of furniture.

The Three-Legged Stool of Knowledge

The "Three-legged Stool of Knowledge" is an important concept to illustrate the three sources of information you need to survive and succeed in the business. Nearly all of the agents who fail do so because they only gather information from the first two legs of the stool. Fortunately, you are not going to repeat their mistake.

The Real Estate Schools

The first leg of the Stool of Knowledge is provided by the

traditional Real Estate Schools and the formal education that they deliver. Those schools provide a valuable service because you cannot get a license without them. They teach the technical information you need for that purpose. Their objective is limited to providing specific formal classes, which usually result in some sort of official reward like fulfilling licensing requirements or earning continuing education credits. They are very good at delivering that much-needed information.

> *Structured learning is not a substitute for experience but it is a great way to gather information and professional designations; you know... all those capital letters behind our names.*

If they were to share some of the things you will learn in this book, they might actually discourage some of their potential students from going into the business and therefore chase away their own customers. That would be contrary to the school's basic mission and self-destructive.

Furthermore, they have no way of knowing who will make it and who will not. The flashy fellow in the front row may have a $1,000 suit and look very promising, but he might have the personality of a pickle or lack the perseverance to survive. On the other hand, the young woman in the corner may be wearing blue jeans and seem distracted, which does not especially boast of success, but she might actually hit it big.

Managers and Sales Trainers

The second leg of the Stool of Knowledge is offered by sales trainers, including managing brokers and other experts. The managing broker provides priceless information about office policies, organizing your files, and marketing. They frequently hold sales meetings and teach things like telephone techniques, hosting an open house and how to show homes effectively.

You can also attend seminars of selected experts and learn more advanced techniques on specialty topics such as how to improve your time management skills, making dynamic listing presentations and advanced closing techniques. Sometimes you get certificates or continuing education credits from these people, and you usually get valuable information and excellent motivational aid. Generally, these folks don't have time to explore all the odds and ends you need to know because they are experts on specific topics.

JOKE TIME - A grieving family is called into the surgeon's office to discuss the dire circumstances of their senile grandfather. The surgeon says to the family, "There is bad news and good news. The bad news is that Grandpa's brain is gone and he will never be the same. But, the good news is he is a perfect candidate for a brain transplant." The surprised family talked among themselves and then one of them asked the doctor, "How much will a new brain cost?" The doctor responded, "It is $100,000 for a typical brain or $5,000 for a Realtor brain." Stunned, the family member inquired, "Why the big difference?' and the surgeon responded, "Everybody knows Realtors are only worth about five percent."

So, that leaves the third leg of the Stool of Knowledge, which is "Experience." You might call it "Insider's Wisdom." Prior to this book, experience could only be gained the hard way: by years and years of trial and error in the proverbial School of Hard Knocks. But that takes too long. Many new licensees do not have time to lose so they want to gain their knowledge from some sort of crash course. This is what Uncle Dave has to offer you. I sincerely believe that reading this book will provide the reader with the equivalent of several years of experience.

This elusive information comes from a blend of personal observations of hundreds of brokers plus real experiences, facts, mistakes, opinions, anecdotes and some occasional juicy gossip is thrown in. Most importantly, I share with you how these things relate to the traits you might have so that you can exploit your strengths and improve your weaknesses before you ever get into your first real estate office.

After a few hours with this book you should have a much better idea of the Insider's Wisdom that is stored in the soul of the successful agents. The knowledge you gain from this leg of the stool will round you out so that your stool won't fall over as has happened to millions of licensees before you. You don't have to be like them. In the next chapter we will see why you have more than enough opportunities to be successful, provided you gather the right knowledge and then put that information to work. But first, here is a true story about my very first real estate transaction. Look for clues that will serve as a source for your first dose of Instant Experience.

Uncle Dave's True Story #1: The Three Stooges of Investing

My very first transaction took place seven years before I obtained my license. When I was twenty-one years old, I joined forces with two long-haired friends to buy some raw land as an investment. Curly, Moe and I each brought a different asset to an inexperienced but enthusiastic partnership.

Curly's dad found a piece of raw ground that was for sale. It was priced well and offered particularly good terms. It consisted of two nice residential lots in a charming mountain community, nestled in the foothills fifteen miles west of Denver. I was aware of his father's successful investments so I did not hesitate to accept the wise man's recommendation.

Moe had a nice free and clear car which we pledged as collateral for a loan. The proceeds of that loan were used as a down payment for the property, and the owner financed the remainder of the purchase price.

I was the only one who had a banking relationship and any established credit, so I was the primary signer for both of the loans.

We all were excited about the idea of investing, but we lacked any real experience. One of our biggest mistakes was a failure to understand a concept I later came to identify as, "completing the circle." More specifically, whenever you buy any property you had better have a good idea what your goal is, as well as an exit strategy. But, we were so focused on profit potential we never even considered that someday we might want to get out from under the property. Therefore, we did not have any idea how we were going to complete our circle.

After we bought the lots, we were proud to be land owners, so we did the only thing we were all good at. We drove to the mountains on weekends and played Frisbee. A few months went by, and then we got a surprise phone call.

A man moving into the area from California was driving around the subdivision when he discovered our lots. Somehow, he got our number and made us an offer to buy the property for a nice profit. That was a minor miracle, because we were doing absolutely nothing to market the land. There was no For Sale sign in the yard. We had not talked to any Realtors. We hadn't even considered reselling the property.

The details are a little fuzzy now because so much time has passed, but I still remember that my share of the profits was $900. At the time, I was earning something like $6.00 per hour working in the local grocery store, so all that "easy money" seemed like millions to me. I was immediately hooked on investing and I still love it to this day.

Think about it. What did you learn?

Hint: Consider the admitted error and how the transaction was structured.

Go to page 215 for your Instant Experience.

Chapter 2 – BELLYBUTTONS or OPPORTUNITIES
or
Choosing Success

You will do well in real estate if you can bake a cake while playing the drums and jumping on a pogo stick, all at the same time. Okay, things aren't actually that hectic, but the basic concept holds true. A skilled broker usually has a handful of transactions in the fire at any given moment.

Multi-tasking is a priceless skill for real estate agents. Other simple skills also pay dividends. Anyone who has ever held a garage sale, done telemarketing or collected signatures for political issues already has a valuable skill: a willingness to talk to people. Have you ever asked anybody for a date? Do you ever explore your disagreements with logical debate rather than emotional rants? If so, you can be an effective communicator. These are the types of skills that help average people to succeed in our business. And it is the fantastic variety in the workday that makes real estate sales such a fascinating way to make a living.

> *Selling real estate is simple. The trick is to identify a specific market and convince those people they ought to work with you. You can even do most of your marketing by mail or email; but you cannot succeed if you sit around and hope the business comes to you because it rarely will.*

If the above information was all there was to consider, there would certainly be reason for beginners to be optimistic about their chances of success, but if selling homes was that easy the survival rate would be much higher. So, let's look at a few other facts, just to give you a better picture of how difficult or easy this journey might be for you.

Who's Really Making It?

In a recent letter which I received from Jennifer Clay of the Colorado Real Estate Commission, she established that her state has nearly 50,000 licensed brokers. Of those, approximately 25% of them are no longer active and a similar percentage let their licenses expire each year. Other states verified similar fatality rates. If we nationalize those numbers, it is estimated that nearly a half-million licensees come and go each year. Now, let's look at a different picture.

There are more than two million licensed agents in our country and one million two-hundred thousand of them, more or less, are members of The National Association of Realtors (NAR).

According to an article on NAR's Webpage dated September, 2008, a typical Realtor completes approximately ten transactions per year wherein they represent either one buyer or one seller. This suggests the average Realtor makes a respectable income of $40,000 to $80,000 per year, depending on local home prices and other factors. But "average" is the operative word in that statement.

A common theory in the sales industry is called the "eighty-twenty rule." It suggests that eighty percent of the sales are made by twenty percent of the salespeople. Uncle Dave's experience confirms that concept. In 2007, approximately 30 percent of all Realtors did not complete a single sale, but one fellow I know completed 178 transactions in that same "off" year. WOW!

What this tells us is licensed selling is a lot like athletics or the entertainment industry. A few folks at the top are making incredible livings, and a whole bunch of agents enjoy a nice comfortable lifestyle. That leaves a substantial number of brokers to wrestle for whatever is left over; those are the ones who give up each year.

Not like these folks!
Laurie, Don, Dale and Earl all had great potential, but none of them lasted a year. They all had the same problem. Once they obtained their license, they didn't want to make any mistakes, so they played it safe and avoided activities that might draw attention to their lack of experience.
So, they waited and waited and waited for the business to come to them. That was their biggest mistake of all. Sadly, that approach sealed their destiny. Worse yet, their story is repeated by hundreds of thousands of new licensees every year. But not you!

You Can Do Well

If all this sobering information discourages you from joining our ranks, please remember the lesson of the Ingress to this book. Specifically, most of the successful agents are ordinary people, probably a lot like you. So, keep reading. Just because some people struggle is no reason you have to suffer the same outcome. You just have to make smarter choices than they did.

To keep things in perspective, let's review some reasons for optimism. Consider these points:

- If Uncle Dave can do well, with all his shortcomings, you can too.

- If you were a high school C student, you are just as likely to be in the top 20 percent of agents as your classmates who were A students.
- People with no college education do just as well as college graduates.
- There is no easier business for ordinary people to make big money quickly.
- You can earn as much money as entertainers—without any special talent.
- You can earn as much as business owners—without all the front-end expenses.
- You can earn as much as drug dealers—without all the risk.
- If you merely want to make a comfortable living, you will be happy to know there are hundreds of thousands of Realtors doing exactly that. You can too!

Perhaps you find all of that general information to be compelling, but you still wonder how it specifically applies to you. In a moment we will take a look at some individual profiles to observe where you fit in and whether this business is well suited to you, but before we do that let me ask you an interesting question.

Discrimination Is Fine with Uncle Dave

Can you identify a very common real estate situation in which numerous people are victims of discrimination for no reason other than that someone dislikes their gender, race, religion or some other distinction? Here is a hint for you. It happens all the time and it is perfectly legal. Give up? That situation arises when members of the public decide which broker they wish to hire.

Discrimination is a normal part of this business and Uncle Dave does not mind!

All agents fall victim to some sort of discrimination if they are in the business for long enough. Uncle Dave is no exception. One time I was holding an open house and a nice female buyer liked the home but made it very clear that she would not retain any male Realtor. She found a female broker whom she liked and we all put the transaction together. Another time, I lost a listing because a widow rejected me in favor of a female broker. I lost a different listing because I drove a modest American car and not a Mercedes like the fellow who was retained. Those are just a few of the ones I know about.

I am certain I lost business because of other things throughout my career. When I first started out, I probably lost business because I was too young. By the time I retired, somebody else probably thought I was too old. Somewhere along the way I might have lost business because I was too fat, too white, too bald, too ugly, too this or too that.

Like it suggests in the box that follows, none of that bothers Uncle Dave because each customer is entitled to select an agent of his or her choice. It would be ridiculous for me to assume that I am better for every single person, in every single situation, every single time. Fortunately, Uncle Dave never had to be that good and you don't have to be that good either. For every person who doesn't want to work with you, there will be somebody else who does.

If a transaction falls apart, try not to take it personally. You are responsible to people but you are not responsible for them.

If I have not yet convinced you that the deck is stacked in your favor, review the categories below. You will fit into at least one of the groups and you will soon discover that people just like you are doing very well indeed.

The Women Working in Real Estate

This section starts off on a very high note. According to one study by the National Association of Realtors, nearly 60 percent of the membership is comprised of our female friends.

A theme of one of my radio programs was, "Women in Real Estate." At the time, RE/MAX was a very powerful force in our area (they still are) so I obtained the state-wide rankings at the end of that year. The number one commission earner in Colorado was an extraordinary woman out of Boulder. It was no fluke, either. She had been among the top earners for several years in a row. Furthermore, six of the top ten spots were taken up by female dynamos. The same indicators were everywhere. In our particular office there were plenty of successful ladies. In a more recent national example, two of the top three RE/MAX agents are women.

When it comes to women in real estate and comparing obstacles to opportunities, we have to conclude that women cannot use gender as an excuse to justify sub-par accomplishments. There is too much evidence of their collective success to allow that.

The Men Working in Real Estate

As stated earlier, the National Association of Realtors (NAR) has more female members than males, but there is an interesting twist to that story. NAR serves the needs of residential agents especially well, but there are also a lot of nonresidential positions. Who do you suppose dominates that group?

One of Uncle Dave's friends works at CB Richard Ellis, the largest commercial brokerage house in the world. One afternoon, we reviewed the agent roster in several markets; the trend was indisputable. More than 90 percent of the sales jobs were held by males. The women held some of the sales positions and there were a fair number of them who had chosen to be licensed assistants or project managers but most of those positions were also held by fellows. I asked my friend why the percentages were so disproportionate and he said that women simply don't seek the jobs.

Just because the guys do well in commercial real estate is no reason to assume they have any problem landing their fair share of the residential transactions. Uncle Dave knows hundreds of male brokers and I have never heard one single complaint that there is some conspiracy or special obstacles holding men back. When we add up all the residential transactions in which men are involved and then throw in all the commercial business they pick up, we have to conclude that they enjoy just as many opportunities as the ladies do.

JOKE TIME - Three boys are in the school yard bragging about whose father is the fastest. One boy says, "My dad is a jogger. He is so fast he can shoot an arrow and catch it before it hits the target." The second boy says, "That's nothing, my dad is a police officer. He is so fast he can fire a bullet at a criminal and push the criminal out of the way before the bullet gets there." And the final boy says, "Your fathers are slowpokes. My dad is a real estate agent and he is so fast he can spend his commission checks before he even gets them."

Earlier, I told you about a widow who invited me to discuss selling her home. I did my homework and gave an excellent presentation. I showed her exactly what we needed to do to get her top dollar for her home. I showed her great examples of places she could move to. I covered everything and covered it well. But I lost the listing.

A few months later I met the Realtor who got that listing. She told me that the widow picked her over me because I was not sensitive enough. As it turned out, the widow was still mourning her husband's death and the entire process meant she was losing her home, not just selling a house. She had a lifetime of memories in her home and it was very painful for her to leave all that behind. Naturally, she was correct. I would have gotten a lot farther with a heartfelt hug than a bunch of numbers. I gained a priceless lesson from that failure and I was much more sensitive to the "feelings" of all people after that.

Young People Working in Real Estate

One of the all-time best trainers of real estate sales techniques is a fellow by the name of Tom Hopkins. By his mid-twenties he was setting sales records. By his late 20s he was one of the most sought-after speakers on the subject of closing real estate transactions. SELL, SELL, SELL! His success is legendary. Obviously, I highly recommend his work for new licensees or anybody else who wants to get juiced up.

> *There are two ways to get the tallest building on the block; one is to build the tallest building and the other is to tear down all the other buildings. Don't be discouraged by small-minded people who try to tear you down so that they look better by comparison.*

On a more personal level, Billy had one of the most impressive starts Uncle Dave ever observed. He nearly dropped out of high school, but his uncle (not me) owned a property management company and gave Billy a job when the youngster was seventeen. Billy took to that work like the proverbial duck takes to water. He got his license when he was eighteen and never looked back. Billy has enjoyed years of success in that corner of the industry. Uncle Dave admires people like Billy.

NAR regularly releases articles acknowledging the exceptional accomplishments of agents under 30 years old. Some of the reasons they do so well are: 1) they know lots of people who are of prime home-buying age; 2) they are not as likely to be distracted by health issues; 3) they tend to have stamina; and 4) most of them stay up with technology. That is a very powerful list.

Whenever Uncle Dave visits real estate offices it is

immediately obvious there are plenty of young agents who are capable of great success.

Once again, there are so many young people doing well you are mistaken if you suppose that somehow things will be tougher for you than some of the others. You simply have too many opportunities to make a believable case.

> *Excuses are like belly buttons. Everyone has one.*

The Mature Brokers

Scores of people respect the wisdom and life experiences you bring to the table. In addition, there are several excellent niches available to you if you wish to focus on them. For example, as your peers advance in years, their children become prime home-buying age and you can pluck off those referrals. Another situation comes up after the children move out, and the empty-nesters (parents) seek alternate housing arrangements for themselves: Some of their solutions are found in condos, senior communities, smaller homes with smaller yards, and areas with warmer climates.

> *There are special professional designations for any broker who wishes to work with seniors. See www.realtor.org/education/ realtor_university/designation*

Other folks want to buy second homes and there are all sorts of opportunities for you among that group. Then there are those who need more medical attention. Once they can no longer use their homes, you are well qualified to help them sell their homes and make the transition. Naturally, these are not your only opportunities for you. You can attack any of the other business that appeals to you, but you cannot deny there are certain situations that bring you extra prospects. The bottom line is those few extra wrinkles you have are a badge of honor. You can use them if you want to, but do not try to tell us you cannot succeed in the real estate industry. Uncle Dave knows way too many mature brokers to accept that excuse.

Working With Your Race, Religion, or Other Classification

If you are a member of any of these groups, you probably realize Uncle Dave is not going to let you off the hook either. There are plenty of opportunities for you.

Obviously, there is nothing wrong with taking advantage of these specialties if you want to. Agents who are bi-lingual can easily find clients who will appreciate their skill. If you are African American or Jewish, there are plenty of people who will love to work with you. If you are gay or single or short you can consider yourself special and use your profile as a big personal bonus if you want to. The choice is yours. Make excuses or make a fantastic living. Once again, the opportunities you have exceed any problems you might face.

I like this observation that Peter made: "It may be just one transaction among many to you, but it is the only one that matters to them. Regardless of who you are working with, you will know more about the business than they do. If people are resisting you it may be because you are going too fast. Slow down and give them the attention they deserve."

As you can tell from the above examples, the real estate industry is filled with lots of fabulous opportunities and a few obstacles for each of us. This is the type of observation that comes directly from that third leg of the Learning Stool. Some people allow themselves to fail and then seek to justify their shortcomings by claiming they are the wrong gender, age or race; but the successful brokers don't have time for such nonsense. They know they can succeed regardless of their profile. You are reading this book because you want to be in the latter group and Uncle Dave knows you can do it.

Now that you have decided not to make excuses, you are ready to learn how your great attitude will affect your lifestyle. We will explore that information in the next chapter, but first here is a true story that might help you avoid some beginners' mistakes.

Uncle Dave's True Story #2: A Cellar Dweller Feller

You never know when you will be confronted with a Fair Housing issue. It may be hard to believe but my very first transaction as a licensed agent was exactly that. I started out in the sales department of a small property management company. I had only been licensed a few weeks when a call came in from a young Hispanic girl who lived with her family in a nearby government-operated housing community. After our receptionist figured out what the youngster wanted, the call was handed to me. The soft-spoken caller told me her mother had saved enough money for a down payment to buy an entry-level property and they wanted to know what to do. Naturally, I was thrilled to help them.

The problem was that I did not speak any Spanish and neither of the parents spoke English. However, all three of the children were bilingual and the oldest one, the caller, was about 17 so I figured she could communicate effectively. Eventually we found a very simple two-bedroom home, which seemed like a castle to them because they were accustomed to living in cramped apartment buildings.

After the closing the parents took one bedroom and the two girls shared the other one. The son was about thirteen years old and he was anxious to take over an old cellar which had been converted into a small non-conforming bedroom. It was tucked under the main floor and it was just a few feet from the old boiler. After the transaction was completed, they were so happy I really got a warm feeling knowing I helped them share in the American dream.

A couple of weeks later I was driving by on one of the nearby cross-streets, and noticed the fire department at their home on an emergency call. One of the firemen told me the boiler overheated and cracked, spilling steam all over the place. He said that nobody was hurt but the young fellow, whose room was in the cellar, was shook up for a while.

The good news was the only damage was to the lost boiler. The bad news was a new boiler would cost them as much money as their original down payment which took them several years to save up. I told my wife about the situation and she said the same thing she always says in cases like that. We called up a heating contractor and had him install a new boiler at our expense. We never did tell them where it came from, but we have been repaid for our efforts many times since then. I am sure they settled in just fine, but unfortunately that was my last contact with that fine family.

Think about it. What did you learn?

Hint: Consider the relationship after the closing and perspectives and unsafe properties.

Go to page 216 for your Instant Experience.

Chapter 3 – INDEPENDENT CONTRACTOR ON CALL
Or
Your New Lifestyle

To begin this chapter, Uncle Dave asked his teacher friends to survey their students of various ages. The topic: What do you want to be when you grow up? The research revealed that one first-grader wanted to become a super hero, another hoped to become a pirate, a third one intended to be a cowgirl, and another hoped to become an art detector—whatever that is.

By the time youngsters got to the 6th grade they had a better grasp of the topic. The most common career choice among boys was athletics, while many of the girls liked singing and dancing. But there were still some interesting choices. One 11-year-old wanted to be a knife thrower; another wanted to work at eBay.

As they reached the threshold of adulthood their choices were more thoughtful. One 12th grader hoped to manage a Lowes Home Improvement Center. Another said he wanted to be an orthopedist because they only work three days per week; another wanted to become the next Dr. Phil. The most common choices were athletic trainers and doctors.

The point of my survey was to prove that nobody picks real estate as their first career choice. Your trusty Uncle Dave has only known a few people who entered the real estate business prior to age 25, and all but one of them tried something else first. I was 17 when I discovered that a career in real estate was for me, but it took 10 years and a handful of jobs before I obtained my license.

A career selling real estate is usually a fall-back choice because it does not fit the mantra we are fed as we grow up. If you were like me you were told to mind your leaders, do well in school, graduate from college, get a good job, marry somebody special and then you would live happily ever after. I tried that, but it did not work for me (except for marrying somebody special).

The problems with the format of yesteryear are plentiful: college is expensive and time-consuming; there is very little job security anymore; working for others is limiting; and, the box called "normal" is boring and unnecessary. All that baggage is unappealing to many ordinary people.

> *Selling real estate is usually a fall-back career because it does not fit the mantra we are fed as we grow up.*

Selling real estate is a great alternative for those who discover they want success without the expense and time chasing ungratifying credentials. But there is an unexpected price to pay for those renegade ways. The cowboy-like lifestyle quickly affects both our professional and personal lives.

Changes in Your Professional Life

The Collective Image Problem

One of the first things you have to understand is you are about to join a group with a substandard reputation, just like politicians, used-car salesmen, and attorneys. But things are not always what they seem. Collectively, politicians have very low approval ratings, but the majority of voters actually like their own elected officials (after all, they voted for them).

We think used-car salesmen are all out to fleece us, but I have met several very nice people in that industry. We accuse attorneys of being over-priced ambulance chasers, but we value their services when we need them.

As far as real estate agents are concerned, the public tends to think we are a bunch of money-grubbing thieves who will say or do anything to make a fast dollar. The irony is many of those same people will gladly list their properties for sale at over-market prices in hopes we can fast-talk some unsuspecting buyer into overpaying for them.

In spite of our professional image, most established brokers are exactly the opposite of what the public perceives us to be. We do not consider our clients and their families to be cash registers waiting to be robbed. We care about people because we value referrals and long-term relationships. Most agents have lots of loyal customers, but that would not be possible if we neglected the people we meet.

> *Those same people who malign realtors will gladly list their properties at over-market prices in hopes we can fast-talk some unsuspecting buyer into overpaying for them.*

Chances are you have never been so disliked and loved at the same time but that is one of the things that make this business so interesting. If you can accept the fact that some people are going to incorrectly prejudge you, you will also be able to accept the other oddities in your new professional life.

Independent Contractor vs. Employee

Some of the differences in your new professional life come from your independent contractor status. When you work for somebody else, you are usually considered to be an employee, but now you are essentially self-employed.

You will notice a big difference in your compensation package. If you are like most of us you will be on a straight commission arrangement. As an employee, your income was steady and reliable like a merry-go-round but now your income will be more like a roller coaster, with some slow uphill climbs and some exciting paydays as a reward.

One drawback to your new arrangement is the absence of a benefits package. Almost all jobs offer benefits including paid vacations, overtime, sick days, paid holidays, health care, opportunities for advancement, profit sharing and other perks. Commission sales offers very few such benefits.

> *Some people will blame you when the market goes against them; others will give you the credit when the market helps them out. However, we are not responsible for either. We don't make the market, we just work in it.*

However, if you take this job seriously, you will make a lot more money than you would if working for somebody else. You can afford to buy your own health insurance and fund a savings account and go on vacations. If you want a raise, you don't have to ask anybody. All you have to do is start a new marketing program or improve your referral system or make some similar adjustment in your workload.

Freedom for Responsibility

You will discover there is more freedom and more responsibility than there is for an employee. You are free to go surfing or to the dentist or to watch your kids play soccer. You can take Thursdays off if you want to or you can work extra-long hours if you are in the middle of a project and don't want to stifle your momentum. One heavy hitter I know likes to take off the third week of every month.

If you aren't especially organized or tidy, you are free to be a slob now. There were always a few of those where Uncle Dave worked. You can specialize in first-time buyers, sellers only, investors, or any area you choose. You can work from home if that fits your needs.

I always liked the fact that I could wear whatever I wanted. Whenever I met somebody I did not know, I utilized the advice of my associate, Peter: "If, they don't know you, the first meeting sets the tone for the relationship, and the final meeting leaves the lasting impression, so dress professionally in those two occasions, but you can dress more casually all the rest of the time." Very few employees have flexibility like that.

> *Down deep, Uncle Dave is a blue jeans and T-shirt kind of fellow. I made a lot of money wearing casual clothes and driving around in pickup trucks.*

But there are added responsibilities too. You will have to abide by all sorts of new rules, regulations and laws, such as the Fair Housing Laws. If one of your deals crashes, you are just out of luck. If something goes wrong, the problem is all yours. You are responsible for all of your own mistakes and some of the problems that are not your fault. If a seller does not give possession when he or she was supposed to, your buyer will expect you to get it worked out. If a buyer refuses to sign his or her papers, your seller wants to blame somebody and you are in the cross-hairs.

The Drama Train

You will also find more drama as a self-employed person. You get to take credit for your accomplishments but you cannot avoid the responsibility if things don't work out. You will feel a hole in your heart if you fail to keep in touch with your friends and then you find out they listed their home with somebody else.

> *The role of an independent contractor is a lot like the life of a parent. You are the ultimate authority and responsible for the outcome, good or bad.*

There are higher highs and lower lows in your income stream. Uncle Dave has observed hundreds of examples of brokers earning $30,000 in a single month. Naturally it is exciting to make more money in one month than other people make in an entire year, but there is another side to that coin. Many new licensees never complete a single sale and there are plenty of bankruptcies among the ranks, mostly for the people who never learn the lessons of this book.

The Added Expenses

It is also difficult to adjust to all the new expenses you will have as an independent contractor. It normally requires a couple thousand dollars just to enter the starting gate: real estate schools, state exams, licensing fees, Errors and Omissions insurance, and Association Dues are waiting for payment. Some of the big franchises also have start-up fees and expenses for training.

You will probably have to take continuing education classes and most of those cost money. You will also want to get better on your own so you will go to breakfast meetings and seminars plus buy books and DVDs. You may wish to earn professional designations and all that specialized training takes away your precious dollars.

> *If you like to sleep in, you'll love being an independent contractor.*

Marketing is gonna cost ya. In some companies you will pay for all your own advertising, business cards and printing plus lock boxes and signs. If you take a client to lunch, you will probably pick up the tab more often than you did as an employee. If you want to put your name on a bus bench or put out a mass mailing, get out your check book.

Naturally, that is a costly package that you did not have as an employee; or did you? The truth is employees have to cover their overhead too. Most businesses take all the costs of running their business into consideration before they settle on how much they can pay their employees in wages.

Therefore, even though your new-found expenses seem high, you should be able to cover them all if you do the simple things laid out in this book.

Finally, there is a silver lining in that cloud of expenses. The IRS allows you to deduct all those costs, so they are effectively paying a nice chunk of it for you. Depending on your income tax bracket, they will refund approximately one-third of actual costs.

Prestige and Professionalism

You will feel more important than you did as an employee. Your friends and family will seek your advice. You will attend marketing meetings and learn about inventory, which will change the lives of people who matter to you. If you elect to join the Association of Realtors (usually recommended) you will abide by a Code of Ethics (always recommended) which will give you a sense of professionalism. You will become involved in community issues and should be a better citizen for it.

> *If your employer is paying you $40,000 per year, you are probably worth more than that; otherwise they cannot justify paying you that amount. So, if you are worth more than that, why do you work for less? As an independent contractor, you will be paid what you are really worth.*

Finally, you might learn to say "Realtor" correctly. It amazes me how many people mispronounce that word, even people who have been in the business for a long time. Look at the spelling closely: R-E-A-L-T-O-R. REAL plus TOR. There is no vowel in the middle. Think of it this way. You do not go to a doc-i-tor and you do not go to a real-i-tor. You are a "Realtor," not a "Real-i-tor." <u>This is one of the easiest things you can do to elevate your professionalism RIGHT HERE AND NOW!</u>

The employee has a relatively boring professional life compared to the independent contractor. They come in, punch the clock, do what is expected of them, watch the clock, punch out and go home. Some people like it that way. Their needs are simple and their job provides the vehicle to obtain the things they want and need.

But things are much different for independent contractors. Their professional lives are a lot like the life of a parent. There may be isolated moments where you are not engrossed in important issues but you are always "on-call."

Changes in Your Personal Life

Some of the benefits and drawbacks that you experience in your professional life will spill over into your personal life. The best example is the "freedom for responsibility" trade-off. This dynamic old-school concept impressed my wife and me so much we applied it as the guiding principle of our child-raising at home.

Perpetual Promotion

Licensees have an extra purpose that is lacking for traditional employees. Everybody you meet matters on a new level. You will constantly seek opportunities to promote yourself, your clients and your products, and not just verbally.

You will buy business cards by the thousands and try to give them all away. All of your correspondence, phone calls and emails lend opportunities for you to toot your horn. I suggest you get a tag line, niche or specialty. Uncle Dave obtained the trade name, "Let's Talk Real Estate," which I used on my radio show, and in all written correspondence. Other brokers have similar catch phrases that they use on Christmas letters, personal stationery, check book and their Web sites.

In addition to selling yourself, you need to be at-the-ready to promote your listings and buyers. Even if the person you are talking to does not know where you can get a buyer for your listing, the listener will recognize that you really do promote your clients and products. The next time they know somebody who needs a good agent you stand a chance of getting a call.

Under the Microscope

People will be judging you differently. Your clothes, your car, your overall appearance, and everything you do matters more than before. Your mannerisms, demeanor, sense of humor, punctuality, vocabulary, accessibility and professionalism all play a role in your success. You are on display, so be prepared.

Uncle Dave wanted to make a good living but I did not like rigid routines or excessive hours away from my family, so I had an informal flexibility policy. I recognized that a high percentage of residential clients must do their housing business on nights and weekends.

Therefore, I decided I would willingly work those hours whenever the circumstances presented themselves. However, on those occasions when I caught myself borrowing too much quality time from my personal life, I tried to pay back that time by taking off a similar amount of other quality time. My personal life was just as important to me as my professional life, so I never had trouble finding a little time to kick back and recharge my batteries.

Your Life at Home

Some of your closest relationships will evolve if you become a real estate agent. Your spouse and children will not have exclusive access to you. An important phone call is always just around the corner. You may have to work weekends or you might suddenly acquire an exciting lead and have to reschedule other activities to attend it. Your cell phone will ring at inopportune times. These things are a regular part of the agent's personal life, but they rarely happen to employees.

Other Relationships

Some of your friendships will be affected. While former friends might resent your income or your constant trolling for business, new friends will find you interesting. All this attention can be exciting.

Whenever you are at a social event like a party or after church, people will want to talk to you about their home, the market or other hot topics. While the "normal" folks are enjoying themselves, you are backed into a corner and talking shop.

One of the painful things that will happen to you is someone you know very well will list their home for sale or buy a home using some other broker. In these cases, they probably have some hidden baggage they don't want you to know about. Perhaps they had a bankruptcy in the past or very poor credit. Finally, they might secretly doubt your commitment to the industry or your skill level, so they simply do not trust you. The personal lives of employees are not usually subjected to disappointments like these.

Get Out Your Checkbook... Again!

If all the added business costs aren't enough to concern you, here are some new personal expenses waiting for you: You will probably buy more prestigious automobiles and replace them more often. You will be driving more miles and buying more gas, plus making more repairs and upgrading your insurance to cover the higher risk of driving your clients around.

You will probably go out to eat more often, because it is a good way to have quality time with people who can send you business. You may be inclined to update your wardrobe or remodel your home so it is better suited to entertaining. All that self-promoting and mind candy is expensive.

Then there are our friends at the IRS. They will take a greater interest in you than ever before. You have to pay higher Social Security taxes than employees do (figure an extra 7% of your adjusted income). You will probably have to send them quarterly tax estimates and if you don't have the money when you need it, you will be punished with hefty penalties and interest expenses.

> *JOKE TIME - One dysfunctional broker had so many bills he could not pay them all. Then he got a great idea. He refinanced his home and consolidated all his debts. Then he only had one debt he could not pay.*

In the final analysis, the broker's days are much more interesting than those of the typical employee. You will have higher highs and lower lows in both your professional experiences and your personal life. The good news is if you are a self-starter you should make enough money to pay for all your new overhead and have a lot more freedom to enjoy. Successful brokers love being independent contractors. The chances are good that you will love it too. However, if you sit back and wait for somebody to give you instructions, as employees do, Uncle Dave is afraid you are in for some tough times.

> *If you implement the ideas expressed in this book you should make enough money to pay for all your new overhead and you will have a lot more freedom to enjoy.*

If you are enthusiastic about all this freedom stuff then you will enjoy the next chapter, which will tell you about some interesting basic "tools" you need to improve your chances. But first, here is a bizarre true story that reveals just how interesting the life of an independent contractor can be, both professionally and personally.

Uncle Dave's True Story #3: Ungrateful to the Max

I once worked with an entry-level investor named Steve. In that capacity, I found a nice triplex which was a great buy at $90,000 and I was seriously thinking about buying it myself, but it fit his needs very well, so I showed it to him. He liked it a lot, but it was a fairly big step for him, so he was very nervous.

I was confident enough in the property and the market at that time to offer him a buy-back guarantee. I said if the deal did not work out and he wanted his money back, at any time within a year, I would buy the property back from him for what he paid for it. So, he could not lose. That was all he needed. We completed the transaction a few weeks later.

About three months after that, I saw Steve at a party and eagerly asked him how the property was working out. To my shock, he grumbled, "Not very well." Naturally, I wanted to know what the problem was. He explained that right after he bought the property, the washing machine in the laundry room broke. For some reason, he thought I knew that was going to happen, so he was angry with me. Naturally, I had no way of knowing the washing machine was going to clunk out, but there was no reason to dwell on that. Well anyway, it was obvious he was unhappy so I offered to buy back the property as previously promised. Then, another surprise was introduced.

He told me he could not sell the property to me because he had already sold it to somebody else. Naturally, I asked him how he came out. His tone took on a vindictive quality as he bragged that he sold the property for $105,000. I was stunned by the entire exchange. Then I was the one who became indignant, which was uncommon for me because I am usually rather stoic.

I said to him, "Let me see if I have this correct. You bought the property a few months ago. A washing machine went out, so you were upset with me and the deal; then, you sold the building for a profit of $15,000, in just a few months. Is that right?" His tone was unchanged as he affirmed the details. I could not believe my ears. I could not imagine how anybody in that situation would be so ungrateful.

Good manners prohibit me from repeating the exact words I said to him next, but I am glad to report the people who knew us both suggested that if they had made a $15,000 profit in a few months from my efforts they would have been more inclined to kiss my feet than to dwell on a defective washing machine. Oh well, there are none as weird as folks.

Think about it. What did you learn?

Hint: Consider the broker's risks when involved with defective properties.

Go to page 217 for your Instant Experience.

Chapter 4 – TOP TEN TOOLS OF THE TRADE #1
Part One - The Basics

Suppose a lady friend of yours suddenly decides to make quilts. Now suppose she begins by sitting down at a sewing machine and starts attaching scraps of material together. Before long she realizes she needs some better tools. Perhaps her machine is inadequate or she needs patterns or some other deficiency is observed. At that moment, she can either go assemble those critical tools or set her project aside and move on to other things in her life. That is the same plight of new agents.

At this point you should understand that selling real estate is fairly simple. Even so, hundreds of thousands of new agents drop out each year, frequently because they were not sufficiently prepared in the first place. Just like the quilter mentioned above, when licensees come to a crossroads they can either go get the missing tools they need or set their "project" aside. Unfortunately massive numbers of them choose to leave us, prematurely.

> **Your reputation is your most valuable asset. You cannot afford to ruin it with bad habits.**

Fortunately, you do not have to repeat their mistakes because you will already have the tools you will need to succeed. In the next two chapters we will review Uncle Dave's Top Ten Tools of the Trade. Uncle Dave finds it odd that these things are not taught in real estate schools and they are rarely discussed in sales meetings or other places. I am glad you found them.

The best place to begin is at the beginning, so this chapter is devoted to the basics.

The Basics

Brokers who have these essential tools in place when they enter their first office have an infinitely better chance of success than those who do not.

Enough Time (Tool #1)

Most of us have hired someone only to discover that once they acquired the job they were more elusive than an all-star half-back. When they put you off or ignored your calls completely, you quickly determined you would not use them again or recommend them to your friends. It makes one wonder how they survive.

There is a reason this is the first tool to discuss. Referrals are so important in the real estate business you cannot be cavalier when it comes to returning calls and responding to your clients' needs. It is time for you to be ruthlessly honest with yourself. How much time do you really have to commit to this endeavor? Naturally, I think you have a better chance if you can work full-time, perhaps 50 hours per week, for the first year or two. The more time you invest the more experience you gain, and experience is your friend. If you cannot commit that much time it is very important for you to find a way to quickly respond to incoming calls so that you appear as professional as your competitors.

Very few part-timers make any real money in this industry. After all, there are countless full-time professionals who have experience, training and long client lists. Most of them understand how important it is to be accessible and responsive. They even have other brokers or personal assistants to field their calls whenever they take a day off. Why would a customer want to work with you if you are consumed with outside activities and unable to react to their needs as well as the pros?

If you are a housewife, you probably have sufficient flexibility in your daily schedule for this responsibility, but if you hold a primary job that restricts your access to a phone, your inability to respond to the needs of your clients assures problems with all but the most accommodating clients.

When it comes to selling real estate, your reputation is your most valuable asset. You cannot afford to ruin it with bad habits. You need enough time to respond quickly to lenders, title companies, clients, brokers and other professionals. If you cannot devote 30 serious hours per week, Uncle Dave believes you are severely impaired; however, if you can invest the time it takes to succeed, you are off to a great start. Congratulations.

Positive Attitude (Tool #2)

Imagine you go to the grocery store on a busy Saturday morning to pick up a bag of cookies and a few lemons. When you get to the registers there are two cashiers, working side by side. You quickly survey the situation to determine which line to join. You notice one of them is cheerful and interacting with the customers, but the other one appears a bit grumpy. Before you make your choice, you glance at your basket and note the irony. One of them is like your cookies while the other one resembles the lemons. Who do you want to work with: lemons or cookies? Well, the same thing is true of your real estate customers; they are attracted to cookies, not lemons.

With that idea in mind, answer these questions as honestly as you can: How will you feel if a client calls you during family dinner? How do you deal with disappointment? Will your spouse and family be willing to share you with other people? Do you tend to get dramatic when things don't go as you would like? If the answers to these questions make you seem more like a cookie than a lemon, you are headed in the right direction.

Have you ever had a job that goes like this? On Monday morning, you punch in around 8:00 a.m. Before long you are watching the clock to see how long it will be until your first break. As soon as the break is over you keep checking your watch for lunchtime. Upon returning from lunch, you anxiously await your afternoon break. Once that is over, you can't wait to get out of there for the day. At 5:00 p.m. you punch out and think to yourself, "only four more days 'til the weekend."

If you have ever held a job like that, you were like a prisoner "doing time." It was probably difficult to maintain a positive attitude, and you didn't stay there any longer than necessary. Most successful real estate professionals are not "doing time." On the contrary, they usually run out of day before they run out of worthwhile things to do. What a fantastic way to make a living!

The typical real estate career is filled with a roller coaster ride of highs and lows. The high points are fairly easy to deal with, but the lows can be more challenging to overcome. You must be truly motivated to navigate past the endless parade of inevitable problems. If you become immobilized or overly dramatic every time something goes against you, you will simply waste too much needed energy and bring down others around you. But a positive attitude and a few cookies can get you past all of that.

People Skills (Tool #3)

You will need a healthy menu of other people skills to be a good real estate broker. That does not mean you have to be a party animal (although some party animals make a lot of money); it just means that you enjoy serving and interacting with other people. Uncle Dave has known many people who would prefer to work in a warehouse or drive a truck than deal with the public, and that is fine; society needs people like them. But the personality of the successful agent is different. It is filled with a broad range of people skills.

Uncle Dave rarely attended office parties or summer picnics while working at RE/MAX, but I still got along with everybody. Nearly all of my coworkers had their own quirks, which made them interesting. In a paradoxical way, it was this wonderful allowance for individuality that attracted dozens of successful and dynamic agents and which resulted in an office full of team players.

Whenever I recall those days I marvel at the way that interesting group interacted with all people. Each person was unique, but certain people skills were nearly universal among them. You can bet there was an abundance of honesty, fun, camaraderie, trustworthiness, caring, perseverance, good communicating, positive attitude, patience, sincerity, energy, friendliness, helpfulness, responsive attitudes, and similar qualities.

> *It was this wonderful allowance for individuality that attracted dozens of team players.*

If you can honestly say that you enjoy working with the public and have a substantial set of people skills, such as those mentioned above, you will probably fit in very well.

Willing to Sell (Tool #4)

We have all met some very successful high-pressure salespeople but most of us don't like dealing with people like that. You might be relieved to learn that those tactics aren't usually necessary to be a successful broker.

One of my great life-long friends is a fellow named Ivan.

He has been selling alarm systems most of his adult life and he has sold countless large systems to some of the best-known corporations in the country. What makes Ivan so interesting is his style. Ivan is the exact opposite of a high-pressure person. He is a very low-key person and he has figured out how to capitalize on his personality.

Since my friend is not a big talker, he has learned how to ask effective probing questions. By doing that, he lets the other person do most of the talking. Ivan is more likely to ask you, "What are you thinking?" than tell you what he is thinking. He will ask, "What can I do for you?" rather than make a recommendation without being asked for it.

The entire conversation revolves around the clients, so they quickly warm up to Ivan. But the beauty of his style is that he learns everything about them before they know anything about him. Eventually, the potential customer is ready to hear what Ivan has to say. When the time is just right, they listen closely because they like him. Naturally, he is very familiar with his products and since he has also learned so much about his customer, the closing itself is nearly effortless.

There are a wide variety of styles among successful salespeople. High-pressure is one of them, and Ivan's style is the antithesis of that. There is some style well suited to your personality and if you enter the field, a good manager should be able to help you learn what techniques will work well for you. But please be assured you don't have to talk people into things they don't want to do.

Regardless of what your style is, the underlying issue remains: You have to be able to coach people when the time is right. Dirk Zeller said it very well in his excellent book, *Your First Year in Real Estate*, "Without exceptional sales skills, you will have to continue to trade large amounts of time for your income." You don't have to twist arms but you must learn to persuade others and ask for the order. You will need to lead people to decisions and to argue without being argumentative.

JOKE TIME - One day a family was especially happy with the new home they just bought so the parents told each of the three sons to buy their real estate agent a gift. They went to her office and the first little boy, who was very friendly, handed the Realtor his present. She noticed the lad had chocolate on his face so she shook the package and said, "I bet it is candy." She opened the present and she was correct. The second boy, who was very loving, handed her his gift and she remembered that the mom worked in a flower shop so she shook the package and said, "I bet it is pretty flowers." She opened the present and confirmed her suspicions. Finally the last boy, who was rather mischievous, handed her his present and the real estate agent noticed the package was leaking. She remembered that the father worked in a liquor store so she wetted her fingers with the leaking liquid, took a taste, then said to the young fellow, "I bet it is Champagne." The mischievous youngster giggled and said "Nope, it is a kitty."

There are shelves full of worthy books on how to persuade others so I will spare the reader specific information on the topic. But, if you need a starting point, you might find the work of Tom Hopkins, Earl Nightingale or Zig Ziglar to be interesting.

The key point here is you are a salesperson, NOT AN ORDER TAKER. If you wait for your clients to tell you they are ready, you will lose too many opportunities. If you are willing to ask probing questions and leave the order-taking to the fast-food restaurants then congratulations are in order; you have just added "Willing to Sell" to your repertoire.

Attack Apprehension (Tool #5)

Which would you rather do during your first month in the business? 1) Stand on a busy street corner and hand out pencils with your name and phone number on them until somebody says something to you like, "I have been thinking about buying a home. Can we get together and talk about the market?" or 2) Sit down in a quiet, comfortable office and design a new brochure, which you will send to people you know, announcing that you are new in the real estate industry and which asks them to refer you some business? Why?

I have asked many new agents the above question and nearly all of them select number 2. When I ask them why, they suggest it is more dignified or more professional or something like that. So, may Uncle Dave take this opportunity to remind the reader that most new licensees also fail to survive past their first year?

I am not saying that it is imperative to hand out pencils on the street corner, nor am I suggesting there is anything wrong with designing marketing materials. What I am saying is, those two activities symbolize the reasons so few people achieve greatness in our business: Handing out pencils requires the courage to act on an unfamiliar concept, while making a brochure provides a temporary hiding place from fear of the unknown.

One day, my father (I guess that makes him your great uncle) shared with me a little piece of advice. He said, "Everybody makes mistakes but how you deal with those mistakes determines how successful you will be." I understood he was essentially authorizing me to try new things without fearing the risk of failure - provided I learned something useful from the experience.

By the time I reached high school, I was more interested in learning new things than getting good grades so I took classes in typing, shorthand, art and gymnastics even though I was destined to screw up in all of them. My father's wisdom helped me understand the person who is not trying new things may feel safe because he does not have to face his mistakes, but the truth is that the person is not growing. Are you willing to make mistakes?

Let's examine some additional choices that struggling licensees often make. That way you can recognize these misguided activities when you arrive in your new company, but more importantly, you can learn what you should avoid.

Many of the folks who prefer choice #2 above are very comfortable in the office. They spend 20-30 hours per week hanging around because they believe being at work equals actually working. They gladly attend sales meetings and training sessions. They will eagerly go to lunch with you and they are generally fun to be around. They gladly talk shop with other agents in the office. They read the newspaper at work and make plenty of personal calls. They are usually working on a new project (newsletter, mailing list, phone pitch, etc.) that they think has great promise. They love to "play office" and they get along with everybody.

Do you notice what is missing? The answer: Equal effort outside of the office. You do not make a living hanging around the office. Furthermore, you cannot count exclusively on your friends and family to send you enough business to pay all your bills. Therefore, you must offer your services to LOTS of new people. The more time you waste "playing office," the less time you have to meet people who can actually help you to meet your needs. In short, your success will come from outside the office, not within it.

Most struggling brokers are "creative avoiders." They are great at delaying, diverting, waiting, redoing, coffee sipping, lunch going, justifying, refraining and anything else that thwarts awkward moments. Their bright and cheery busywork serves as an effective diversion from their fear. They are so concerned about what other people think of them, they won't do the things that really matter.

The key word in choice number 2 earlier was "comfortable" and people who seek comfort are doomed. What about you? Are you willing to give away pencils on the street corner just to prove you can do something you've never done before, or do you only play it safe? Will you make up a client list and then regularly contact those people or will you sit back and hope somebody feels obligated to call you? Will you call all of your contacts at least four times a year to ask for business or do you assume they would rather not be bothered? Are you willing to take strangers to lunch or would you rather embrace people you already know? Will you knock on a few doors around your new listing in search of other leads or do you prefer to get back to the office?

> **Your success will come from outside the office, not within it.**

If you are the type of person who requires the comfort of familiarity, you should seek employment testing soft lounge chairs somewhere, but if you are a self-starter who has the audacity to attack apprehension by performing tasks that are not immediately comfortable there is a VERY GOOD chance you will find yourself right in the middle of many successful transactions with greatness at your fingertips.

In the next chapter we will observe the more sophisticated tools you need; but before we do that, what can you glean from this true story?

Uncle Dave's True Story #4: Enabled by the Disabled

One of my favorite clients was an organization that provided for the needs of disabled people. Some of their "clients," as they referred to them, had mental disabilities while others were physically challenged. The degree of disability varied widely among the clients. Goods and services were provided on an "as needed" basis, from cradle to grave, regardless of their ability to pay.

One day I was recruited to help them find a community home for some clients who were ready to live in a traditional neighborhood. Even though the task required some extra effort and patience because neighbors can be nervous about having this type of group-home in their community, I welcomed the challenge because I respected the cause.

Eventually, a nice property was located and they bought it knowing they would have a long-term use for the home. I quickly became their only real estate agent and I helped them buy quite a few group-homes as well as rent some other properties for their clients.

Along the way, Uncle Dave learned they were considering finding a bigger office building for their main headquarters. Unfortunately, suitable buildings were usually way beyond their means. After a couple years of casual but ongoing shopping I discovered an ideal 8-story building in a nice central location. The previous tenant was the Federal Government, which had used it for 20 years or so, but the property did not meet its needs any longer. It was slightly outdated by then but still solid in every respect.

I obtained a brochure from the office of the listing broker and went to lunch with my contact so I could inform him of the opportunity, as I did on several previous occasions. They were usually a little slow at getting things done because of their own internal bureaucracy so I saw no need to pester them about the property for a while.

Ten days later I followed up on the issue and discovered that they had already put in a contract on the property and that the contract was indeed accepted. As it turned out, my buddy gave the brochure that I provided him to the president of their group, who, in turn, made a call to the listing broker and the two of them slammed a deal together before anybody else knew what happened. That quickie deal cost me a commission in excess of $50,000.

When my contact realized what happened, he felt awful. Prior to that transaction, he always had authority to make the real estate decisions so he never expected the president would complete such a large transaction without at least keeping him in the loop.

Naturally, I was disappointed on a selfish personal level, but I knew I was their primary agent and I was genuinely pleased that I had played a role in helping them acquire a great building which would serve their clients' needs for decades yet to come. I remained positive and I knew I would never make that mistake again.

My contact appreciated the way I handled the situation. After that, he sent me personal referrals in addition to all their other organizational transactions. One time, I even bought a nice duplex and put an addition on the back of it so it would meet the special needs of some of their selected clients. Then they rented that property from me for 5-6 years. After they moved out, I sold the property and ended up making enough profit to recapture the entire previous loss. Imagine that!

The people in that group knew I was as sincerely motivated to help their clients as they were. They appreciated my positive attitude and that combination cemented a priceless relationship. Years later, when I retired, I donated to them a $40,000 baseball card collection to auction off at a fund raiser. I have also made other contributions to them over the years.

I don't know who the big winner from that relationship was, but I do know my positive attitude and our mutual motivation to serve their clients was at the root of all of it.

Think about it. What did you learn?

Hint: Consider venturing into commercial transactions and how the tools of this chapter were used for long-term success.

Go to page 217 for your Instant Experience.

Chapter 5 – TOP TEN TOOLS OF THE TRADE #2

Part 2 – The Complete Package

Imagine a famous singer such as Carrie Underwood. She is certainly very gifted but singing is not her only talent. I have watched her at several award ceremonies, and she is very charming. She is always humble, happy and likeable. She looks as good as she can; and I bet she has to work like a dog. There are other people who sing as well as she does, but they just don't have such a complete package and their success is limited because of it.

> *Assume that the definition of a housewife is "a married woman whose principal occupation is managing a household and attending to domestic affairs." Given that definition, why would a typical full-time housewife have a better chance at succeeding in real estate sales than her college-educated male counterparts? The answer is coming up.*

The same thing holds true for licensees and especially you. The basic tools mentioned in the previous chapter will take you a long way, just as Ms. Underwood's singing has served her very well, but those tools are not enough to tip the scales in your favor. The good news is you have plenty of special tools that will enable you to complete your package. Once you know what those tools are and how to use them effectively you too will leap to the head of your class.

Uncle Dave is pleased to introduce you to the final five fantastic tools that you need. If you recognize qualities that you already possess or you are enthusiastic about acquiring, you may be at the threshold of your new career; but if these characteristics make you uneasy, significant effort will be needed to overcome any deficiency. Here is some more priceless information from that third leg of the Stool of Knowledge.

Your Support System (Tool #6)

It is widely reported that half of all marriages end in divorce. I have not been able to find any statistics to tell us the divorce rate among real estate professionals, but one seminar speaker claimed it is higher than normal. My own experience tends to agree with him.

Realtors and other real estate professionals have all the same problems everybody else has, perhaps more. Uncle Dave knows of divorces, alcoholism, bankruptcies, affairs, arrests, gambling problems and unexpected deaths, all in one office.

The cause of all this stress can be anything from extended hours, fluctuating income streams, inadequate effort, jealousy, lust for drama, personal issues and social conflicts to anything else. Fortunately, you will understand why it is so important to have a good support system right from the beginning. Here is why.

For starters it takes several months to obtain a license and select an office. Then you have to find some business somewhere. Even if you have an immediate listing or buyer, there is no guarantee you will be able to quickly complete a transaction and receive a commission check. Furthermore, once a contract is executed between your client and somebody else, it will probably take a full month or so to complete the closing process and gain your monetary reward.

If you don't already have a license, it will probably take at least six months to get to your first pay check and there is no assurance of additional income after that, but that is not the worst of it. When you finally do start making some steady money, you have so much overhead and tax liability you are likely to be disappointed in your take-home pay.

As bleak as all that sounds, the reader should be encouraged by the fact that all successful agents found a way to get past those difficult times and Uncle Dave will introduce you to several ways to do it.

One of the best ways to get through that initial period is to start out with enough money in the bank to sustain yourself for six months after you receive your license. If you have a savings account or a boat (or similar asset) which you can sell if necessary, that might be good enough.

Naturally, you could work at some other job, but remember the discussions about enough time in the previous chapter. If you have no other support system, this option should be utilized as a means to generate leads and pay your bills until you get on your feet. Therefore it is best if the other job involves working with lots of other people somehow. A cocktail waitress, a cashier or working at a large company would all be good candidates.

> *Steve is a very successful broker who utilized a cookie route for this purpose. He had to be at his first account by 6:00 a.m. He was able to attend urgent real estate phone calls when he was driving between accounts. He let all the people on his route know that he was in the business and he picked up quite a few leads from them. By 1:00 p.m. Steve was usually done with his route and immediately attended his real estate job. He worked like that for a couple of years after he had his real estate job humming and then he let go of the cookie route.*

Your support might come from a helpful family member or partner who really understands your lifestyle and can deal with it effectively. If your parents or friends are willing to let you live with them until you get your income stream flowing, you have a great benefit.

Another option is available to those who have a spouse or partner who works. It is a lot easier to pay your bills if somebody else is bringing in a paycheck while you gain your footing.

Your support system can come in the form of a safety net. You can avoid the high-risk world of commission sales by securing a salaried position within the industry (see Chapter 13).

Finally, you might be able to borrow some start-up money or obtain a government grant. Simply visit the Small Business Administration's Web site (www.sba.gov) for links to government grants.

A typical full-time housewife has a better chance at succeeding in real estate than her college-educated male counterparts because she is not the primary bread winner in her family. Therefore, if her partner can provide sufficient income to maintain their lifestyle, she has more "staying power" than someone who has to be the primary breadwinner.

Many of the agents who have come and gone never lent sufficient consideration to this topic. Uncle Dave does not want you to join them. If you run out of gas before your career arrives at its destination you might as well avoid the aggravation altogether.

Make certain you know how and why you can make it for at least six months. If you have people or resources you can rely upon to get you through the difficult early months you will have a much better chance at success. This is not the career to begin on a shoestring and a prayer. There is plenty of evidence to prove that.

Your Sphere of Influence (Tool #7)

Nobody knows the exact same people you know. Some people may know your family members; others may know your spouse's coworkers. Still others may know the members of your college sorority and some people might know all the parents of your daughter's Girl Scout troop, but you are the only person who knows all of them.

Those people and all the other people you already know comprise a sphere of influence and they are priceless to you. Your bond with them, either personally or professionally, is what makes them special to you. Generally, they are the people you would recognize and know by name if you happened to see them at the local shopping mall. Since the members in your sphere already know you, most of them will invite or allow access to them. The more they hear from you, the more they will trust you. Once they like you and trust you, they will be enthusiastic about working with you and sending you referrals.

> *You have no greater path to business than through your sphere...*

Peter is the best of anyone I know at working a sphere. Whenever he meets somebody new he promises them he will protect them from common mistakes and he agrees to work hard to help them accomplish their goals. He follows that promise with a requirement he has of them. He tells them in a fun-loving way, "After I dazzle you with my brilliance, you have to thank me, pay me and send me a referral within the next six months." I have watched him do this and he has a unique way of releasing the pressure with his style while making it perfectly clear he really means it. He is so convincing ALL OF THEM AGREE TO IT, or he won't work with them. He reminds them of their obligation when they write an offer and again when they attend the closing. Most of them take their commitment to him very seriously. After that, he does not miss opportunities to remind them, in his own light-hearted way, of their promise. Sometimes, they giggle together at his not-so-subtle reminders. Peter has gobs of loyal clients sending him referrals and he has always made a phenomenal living working his sphere of influence.

You have no greater path to business than through your sphere, so you must be willing to devise a program that will exploit this unique opportunity. In a later chapter we will go into greater detail about how to employ this dynamic tool. If you do it effectively, you may find yourself to be so busy that you can't keep up with all the business. If you are willing to commit large blocks of your time and resources to your sphere of influence, you should do very well.

Your Special Self (Tool #8)

If you are a cowboy, a housewife, a gardener, a car pooler, a political junkie or a biker you have extra opportunities within that set of like-minded folks. All you have to do is take on a "leadership role" among that class. For example, you can become the leader of the PTA, the organizer of the exercise class, the soccer coach or the commissioner of a fantasy football league. If you are religious, you should volunteer for new activities around the church. If you like bowling you should sponsor a bowling team, or better yet, an entire league.

Your common interest with people within that group gives you access to them while doing something that you already like. And, your leadership role among them will earn their respect and help them to remember you when they have an opportunity to send you business.

Another useful idea is to develop a niche that comes naturally to you. You can drive a distinctive car, offer a guaranteed buyout program, always wear a pink sweater, paint tropical fish on your car, become the "Hidden Hills Specialist," or be the pencils-on-the-street-corner lady. Robin promoted herself as a "condo queen." She helped people sell their condominiums and a lot of times she doubled up her commissions by helping them move up into their first single family home. Annie has a tag line. She is the "most responsive agent." She includes her phrase on all cards, mailings, brochures and emails. Almost any niche you claim is worthy, and you are not limited to one such specialty; but you should consider who you are and find a way to capitalize on your established interests.

Systems, Not Deals (Tool #9)

Occasionally a miracle deal will fall into your lap, but you cannot make a living off of haphazard deals; instead, you need good systems.

There is a big difference between being "in the business" and actually making a living by selling homes. One sales manager I interviewed told me that he has to fire more new agents for lack of action than anything else (hundreds of thousands of agents have this problem). These licensees go through all sorts of effort to obtain a license and pick an employer, but then they sit around the office waiting for something good to happen to them.

Understandably, that lack of systematic effort makes for long boring days. Eventually, these people realize if all they are doing is waiting around for the phone to ring, they might as well do that at home, so they stop coming to the office; thus, they effectively surrender. I suspect that most of those people told a few friends and family members that they were in the business but they did not do much more after that.

One advertising expert I talked with said most people need to hear a message eight times before they really understand it. I see no reason to doubt him. We can also observe that TV commercials are aimed at ten-year-old children. Therefore, advertisers know if they expect somebody to understand a message, they have to repeat that message many times and they have to keep it simple. The same holds true for you. You have to constantly remind your people that you want referrals. They will not remember on their own.

Later in this book we will explore many great systems that you can employ to make your phone ring over and over again, but please be assured if you expect to make a living by just sitting on your butt and waiting for miracle deals to fall into your lap, you will most likely fail. The objective of a real estate agent is to FIND people who want to relocate, then help them do it. It takes good systems, not miracle deals.

If you are not willing to do that, at least burn leaves in your yard and send out regular smoke signals which ask for business: At least you will have regular contact with unhappy neighbors and some firemen and a judge or two.

Financial Discipline (Tool #10)

Regardless of all the great skills you develop or all of the wonderful tools you wrangle up, poor financial practices can destroy it all.

A recent article I read on the Internet suggested that on the average, every single man, woman and child in America owes approximately $3,000 in consumer debt (auto loans, credit cards, student loans and the like, but not real estate loans); but there is more to the story. We know that children don't buy washing machines or lattes with credit cards so we must assign their share of the collective obligations to their parents. Furthermore, half of all households have no such debt, which means the adults in the other half of the homes are responsible for all of that incredible national consumer debt. WOW! Those people can grab their credit cards faster than a gunslinger can draw a six-shooter. Unfortunately, too many agents have similar problems.

Substandard financial habits have cursed many seasoned brokers, and Uncle Dave has known plenty of them. Instant gratification, auto loans, minimum payments on credit cards and maxed-out home loans are common. Sadly, it is just a matter of time before that gut-wrenching feeling of desperation comes a-knocking. They need a check, any check, just to get by. What a king-sized bummer because the entire situation could have been avoided; if only...

New brokers are even more vulnerable to the consequences of cavalier financial practices than the old pro's mentioned above, but if you want to make real estate sales a long-term career Uncle Dave strongly urges you to take this topic more seriously than those people, especially if you are the primary bread winner in your family.

Fortunately Uncle Dave knows a simple three-step philosophy that will solve your financial problems. The system is so simple, most people find it boring. But those who commit to it are well rewarded. In chapter nine, I will share all the details of the dynamic system with you, but at this moment all you need to know is Hate Debt, Save Consistently and Invest Wisely.

JOKE TIME - There once was an elderly woman who died, leaving behind her husband and their middle-aged son. A year later, the son discovered two surprises. The first surprise was that his parents had secretly accumulated an estate worth twenty-five million dollars. The second surprise was that his father was terminally ill and would not live more than a few more months.

The son was still single and never had been very successful with the ladies, but he was confident that once he got his inheritance he could meet and marry a wonderful woman. That evening he came across a perfect candidate at the neighborhood bar. He bought the young beauty a drink and bragged about the large inheritance which he was about to receive. They enjoyed the evening then they traded personal information and agreed to keep in touch.

> *A few weeks later the fellow heard a knock on his door and when he answered it he discovered the beautiful woman he had met at the bar. He was very happy to see her until she said, "Guess what! I am your new stepmother!"*

Anybody can become a financial expert.

You can become a financial expert, too. The important thing to realize is it is more critical than ever to get a handle on your finances. You must approach your resources as any other business person would. Those who implement budgets and stick to them can build fantastic retirement portfolios and accumulate savings accounts to carry them through the tough times. Uncle Dave wants you to be in that group.

How about it? Are you good at handling your finances or are you one of those people who always has some month left over at the end of your money? If you are in the latter group, please take Uncle Dave seriously when he tells you that it is extremely stressful for the folks who never get this issue under control. You will have plenty of drama in your workday without all the extra pressure of a lean purse.

If you have bad money-management habits and are not willing to fix the problem, you should put this book down right now and try something else. No career is worth the aggravation which awaits you.

However, if you already manage your resources fairly well or if you are sincerely willing to live within a disciplined budget, then you will be able to avoid a tragic fate that has befallen countless millions of brokers before you.

As we close out the section regarding Uncle Dave's Top Ten tools of success I would like to remind you that these great tools are of little use without "action." Once again, these things are simple to understand but not necessarily easy to implement. They are not ordinarily taught in other venues, so this information is from that third leg of the Stool of Knowledge.

After the true story below, and the easy chapter behind this one, we will find out exactly what action is necessary to get the most out of these Top Ten tools.

In the meantime Uncle Dave is comforted to know that those of you who can assemble this dynamic group have an excellent opportunity to join the small percentage of brokers who survive for the long term.

Uncle Dave's True Story #5: Beneath the Sister's Habit

When I got my license, I assumed that having six sisters would really pay off. Uncle Dave was licensed less than six months before the first such opportunity presented itself. Margie is a couple years older than I am and she was thinking of getting a bigger home. She lived across town in a typical middle class neighborhood. She let me know what she was looking for and I was excited to have the opportunity to help her. Margie mentioned she had discussed her situation with another broker in her area, but I did not give it a lot of consideration; after all, I was her brother.

Like many other people in her situation, Margie did not want to sell her home until she found a suitable replacement. At the time, I was too inexperienced to understand the best way to handle that situation; so, we got together for several consecutive weekends to look at potential replacement homes in her preferred neighborhoods. We saw quite a few homes and I was confident we would eventually find a suitable property. Then, I got a news flash.

> *Uncle Dave eventually learned that it is just as bad to find the home of your dreams and not be able to buy it because you are still attached to your current home, as it is to sell your current home and not have a replacement property to move to.*

One evening I called Margie to make arrangements to get together on the following weekend. I was surprised to discover that just a few nights earlier the other broker she mentioned had just listed the perfect home for her. She not only had a contract offer accepted on that home, but she even listed her current home for sale with that same broker.

Predictably, I was disappointed because I thought Margie knew how important her business was to me. When I told my sales manager about my loss, he told me that under the circumstances, Margie's actions were completely justified. She was simply looking to move, so she was willing to go with whoever found what she wanted. The other fellow did that, but I did not, so he was the one who got paid. That happens to all of us.

Think about it. What did you learn?

Hint: Consider the Sphere of Influence, buying first versus selling first, and loyalty.

Go to page 218 for your Instant Experience.

Chapter 6 – FANTASTIC QUALITIES YOU AIN'T GONNA NEED
Or
You Are Already Perfect

It is time for a change of pace. For two chapters we have been discussing what you "must have," but this chapter is intended as a fun way to prove there are scores of other great qualities that you don't need at all and, more importantly, to illustrate there is certainly plenty of room for you, no matter how unusual you might be.

To get an idea where you stand, take a brief glance at the list below. Within sixty seconds put a plus sign by ten of the qualities you think apply especially well to you and put a minus sign by five items that seem the most unlike you. Do not get bogged down in analysis. You cannot be wrong. The object is to move quickly. After you have done that, drop down to the bottom of the list for further instructions. Quickly now!

Fantastic Qualities You Ain't Gonna Need

active
active children
adaptable
adventuresome
aggressive
ambitious
analytical
articulate
attractive
authority figure
beautiful eyes
beer drinker
belong to clubs
big family
big-hearted
bilingual
boater
book smart
bowler
bright
care giver
cautious
character
charitable
cheerful
church member
combative
committed
common sense
competitive
concept person
considerate
conversationalist
cooperative
courageous

cynical
dancer
dad
dedicated
detail person
disciplined
dog lover
drinker
driven
early riser
energetic
enthusiastic
entrepreneurial
environmentalist
financially secure
fisherman
flexible
follows directions
forthright
friendly
frugal
fun-loving
gardener
gift of gab
good communicator
good cook
good learner
good net worth
good support system
gourmet cook
grateful
greedy
quiet
hard worker
have enough time

healthy
helpful
high-pressure type
high school graduate
hog breeder
honest
honorable
idealistic
impulsive
independent thinker
inquisitive
insightful
inspirational
instinctive
integrity
interesting
inviting smile
joke teller
kind
knowledgeable
large family
likes reunions
likes garage sales
likes pets
likes seniors
likes sports bars
likes the telephone
lively
loyal
married
mathematical
methodical
mischievous
mom, I am one
mom, I have one

moral
motivated
muscular
musician
NASCAR fan
naughty
negotiator
neighborly
nice
nice car
nice hair
non-drinker
observant
open-minded
optimistic
opinionated
ornery
organized
party animal
patient
people person
perceptive
perfectionist
persistent
persevering
physically fit
playful
poker player
polite
political
positive attitude
practical
pragmatic
pretty smile
promiscuous

provider
prudent
punctual
quiet
quilter
reader
religious
realistic
reliable
recycler
reserved
respectful
resists change
responsible
resourceful
retired
risk-tolerant
romantic
ruthless
secretive
self-control
self-starter
sense of humor
sensitive
serious
sexy
shopper
sincere
single
skier
smart
smoker
smooth talker
snappy dresser
sociable

sports fan
square dancer
stoic
straightforward
street smart
strong
stubborn
studious
successful
supportive
talkative
technology-savvy
television fan
thick-skinned
thorough
thoughtful
tireless
tolerant
traveler
trustworthy
veteran
well conditioned
well groomed
winning attitude
working spouse

After you do that little exercise, review each one of the items you marked with a minus sign. Now, try to imagine how somebody else could actually utilize that item as an effective trait for their own success. For example, your children might be grown up or you may have never had children so you put a minus sign next to "active children." Even though that asset does not apply to you it is fairly easy to recognize that somebody with youngsters has a great opportunity to interact with other young families, and lots of those families move around as their needs change.

JOKE TIME - A smart young Realtor had only been licensed a few weeks when his parents decided to sell their home. The father decided the son needed to "earn" the listing so the father invited the son and a seasoned old broker to his home at the same time to compete for the business. To make things easy for his son, the father made up a test that was filled with 25 easy questions that he thought his son could answer. He then put both agents in the same room and told them that whoever did better on the test would get the listing. When they were done, the father graded the tests and discovered they both missed only one question but it was the exact same one. So the father sat them down and told them what he discovered and announced that he decided to give the listing to the old-timer. The son thought that seemed unfair and demanded a better explanation. The father said, "On question twenty, you wrote 'I don't know' but the old-timer's answer was 'Me neither.'" The son was really irritated and said, "That means he cheated." The father said, "It also proves he will do practically anything to sell my home."

Let's try another one. Suppose you have never considered yourself to be particularly "romantic." Can you imagine how that quality could help somebody else? How about this: Romantic people tend to be in touch with their feelings and people like that should be able to tune into the emotions of their clients.

The point of this exercise is to illustrate that even though there are some common threads among us, we are all very different. Most importantly, you do not need to be somebody or something you are not. On the contrary, the third leg of the Stool of Knowledge has this special message for you: You are perfect, just the way you are. That is why so many agents find real estate to be such a wonderful career choice. I hope you will join us.

Now here is an interesting story for you. It has lots of instant experience.

Uncle Dave's True Story #6: Crooked Profits

Bob's kids were grown and he was divorced by the time Uncle Dave met him. His lack of family ties enabled him to move any time he wanted to, which he was always willing to do—provided there was a sufficient reward for the effort. That worked out great for both of us. Over a ten-year period he bought and sold a handful of homes, plus many investment properties.

> *Nobody ever called Bob or me normal.*

When it came to his investment properties Bob bought a few in his own name, but he preferred to partner up with me. Knowing Bob, I suppose he reasoned that if I was willing to put my own neck in the noose with him, he could assume it really was a sound investment, and if anything went wrong he would have a competent ally. Regardless of his reasons, we worked well together and completed dozens of successful transactions.

One of our interesting adventures came about when I discovered a government-owned foreclosure property that was structurally defective. In certain areas in Colorado there is expansive soil that can force some homes to heave. In the most severe cases, we have observed homes shift off their foundations.

My inspection of the 4-bedroom home on Saratoga Avenue revealed semi-serious cracks in all the cement slabs, including the driveway and the basement floor. There were also visible cracks in the mortar between bricks and under windows on the exterior of the building. The interior of the home also presented problems. There were cracks in the walls, and the doors would not close correctly. Then there were the floors: In one corner the entire home heaved four inches, leaving a very noticeable slope to the floors. There was graffiti on the walls and the home stank of cat pee. Any buyer would have to pay all cash because no lender would make a loan on a home in that condition and only a fool would consider buying a home like that. (You know where this is going, don't you?)

Most agents would consider a home like that to be undesirable in every sense of the word, but Uncle Dave realized that the government had to sell that property and "at the right price" it could make sense. After multiple price reductions, the asking price was a measly $35,000, which was a small fraction of what similar homes were selling for in the neighborhood.

Based on market rents at the time, it was easy to determine that a cash buyer could rent the property out and recover the full purchase price within four years. After that, there was $8,000 per year in cash flow to be enjoyed. I immediately knew I needed to call Bob.

I told him about the house and why I thought it was a "sleeper." When I told him, "Somebody I know is going to buy this property." I then asked, "Would you like to look at it?" Nobody ever called Bob or me normal. We met at the property right after he got off work.

While we were wandering around the house, a lady Realtor walked in the front door to inspect the home for one of her buyers. She was in the home about ten seconds before she literally shrieked, "Oh, my God" and made an instant exit. I am sure she observed the same things everybody else did; a crooked, smelly house. The next morning Bob said, "Let's offer them $28,000." A week later, the government accepted Bob's offer. Bob paid cash for the property and peeled off about $5,000 more for new carpet and paint plus made a few safety and cosmetic repairs. Then we rented out the property.

About a year later Bob decided he could live in that crooked house himself for practically free. Uncle Dave sold Bob's existing home and my bachelor friend lived mortgage-free, for three more years in a 2,200-square foot, four-bedroom, structurally defective family home.

Repeating his pattern, the day came when Bob was ready to move again. We discussed his options and elected to list the crooked home for sale. Since he never repaired the structural problems, financing was still an issue, so we decided Bob should be the lender. We listed the home for $75,000 with owner-carry financing. A week or so into the marketing process, I got a sign-call from Johnnie, the eventual buyer.

Johnnie could not afford many homes and he could not qualify for traditional financing so this home was ideal for him. The agreed price was $68,000, which was half of what other homes in the neighborhood were selling for. The down payment was $10,000. We made out a lengthy and complete disclosure form and required Johnnie to acknowledge exactly why he got such a terrific price. He signed it, without objection.

It was barely one year later when Johnnie suddenly stopped making payments. By that time, Bob had recovered most of his original purchase price from the combination of collected rents plus Johnnie's down payment and the interest Johnnie paid on the loan to that date. And, we must not forget, Bob himself lived in the home, payment-free, for three additional years. Overall, Bob was way ahead.

We discussed Bob's next move. He acknowledged that he liked the monthly income, so he elected to renegotiate Johnnie's loan. He offered to temporarily forgive the amount of the unpaid monthly payments and lower Johnnie's monthly payment. In exchange we added the back payments and a "processing fee" to the unpaid loan. We also raised the interest rate. Finally, we required Johnnie to pay off the loan, in full, within three years. Johnnie loved the solution because of the breathing room it afforded him. Payments resumed and things returned to normal...for a while.

Over the next couple years, Bob made friendly calls to Johnnie to remind him of the obligation to pay off the loan, but Johnnie seemed nonchalant about the deadline. Several months prior to the final due date of the loan there was no evidence that Johnnie was going to meet his obligation. Bob was fed up with Johnnie's shenanigans so he called me to discuss the matter one more time. This time, Bob wanted out.

We observed that the remaining unpaid balance of the loan from Johnnie was about $51,000. I offered Bob $45,000 for his position. He enthusiastically accepted the offer and we completed the transaction a few days later. After accepting my check Bob successfully tripled his money in addition to living mortgage-free for three years, all because of that crooked house.

I was also in a good position: If Johnnie paid the $51,000, as his note required, I would pocket $6,000 for a short-term investment. If he did not pay, I could renegotiate his debt again or foreclose on the property and gain gobs of equity (my last choice). I called Johnnie to inform him I was his new lender. A few weeks later, Johnnie borrowed enough money from one of his relatives to pay me off. A short time after that, he sold the home for a modest profit. Good for him. In the end, we all came out well.

Think about it. What did you learn?

Hint: Consider the basic point of this chapter, the benefits of clients like Bob and the contrast between narrow-minded agents and creative ones.

Go to page 219 for your Instant Experience.

Chapter 7 – YOU WON'T NOT BE NOT DOIN' NOTHIN'
or
What You Will Do

Throughout this book Uncle Dave has reminded you that the real estate business is fairly simple, but not particularly easy. I trust that by now you understand what I meant. I suspect you understand nearly everything we have talked about, even when it was new to you. Now we are going to mix in a few more ideas; many of them address the effort that is necessary. Then you will know what I mean when I say real estate is not particularly easy. If you work full-time and pack your days with these activities you will be more concerned with how to spend all your money than how to merely survive.

Once again, you might uncover information that you find objectionable, but if you can derive pleasure from attending to the details of the industry and digging for treasures you will soon be rubbing elbows with other top professionals. We have already talked about the activities and efforts of struggling agents. Now let's take a look at how successful agents (like you) approach their typical days.

The very first tool we talked about was enough time. This

precious commodity is too valuable to waste, so you need to figure out how to use your time effectively. Naturally, Uncle Dave can teach you how to do that.

> *According to* **The Millionaire Next Door,** *self-employed people make up less than 20 percent of the workers in America but account for two-thirds of the millionaires. Now, you have a realistic chance to join them.*

Your days will be very productive if you approach them as if you were playing a simple three-step game. First you must get organized. Second, you should attend to all of the irons you already have in the fire. Finally, you should shake the trees for new business.

Plan Your Day

Your first priority every day is to lay out a strategy to get the maximum results out of your time. Even if you are instinctively organized, you need to spend a few minutes each day to compile a complete list of all the things you need to do. There are several good ways to do that.

Many agents like Day Planners. You can get one from any office supply store. In essence, they are thick appointment books. The advantage to a Day Planner is you have a complete and easy overview of all your appointments, by date and time, well into the future. But they are bulky, like a purse, and if you lose one or misplace it, the stress is enormous.

> *It takes a lot more than just hanging around the office to succeed. One very important responsibility is to generate leads. But it is not difficult.*

If you are like Uncle Dave, you can design your own "Daily Control Form" that is much less cumbersome. Mine was comprised of a single page and it was designed to assign priorities to tasks of each day so that I worked on the most important things first. That way if one of the items on the "to do" list did not get finished, the consequences were insignificant.

The top 5 lines allowed for Scheduled Appointments of that day. Then, I examined all of my Active Transactions to be certain those deals were moving along as expected. After that I acknowledged Routine Obligations such as paying bills or some sort of prospecting. The final group of entries on the control form is for all of the Odds and Ends. These items can include practically anything, such as wash your car, write a newsletter, get to the beauty parlor, or clean up your desk. Sometimes I listed the odds and ends in order of importance, but other times I wrote a number next to them as a means to identify which items had a higher priority.

That was all there was to it. It rarely took more than 5 minutes to prioritize my day this way. I kept my Control Form with me all day and constantly referred to it. I looked at the very first entry and if it was not time for that appointment, I worked right down the list, in order, knowing precisely which activity was the most important to do next. As the day progressed, I simply wrote new appointments on the back of my form and later transferred that information to a large desk calendar that I kept at the office.

There was very little stress because all the priorities were attended to in a timely way, rather than at the last minute, which seems to be a common practice of some of our co-workers. Furthermore, the risk of loss was nearly insignificant because there are only activities of one day listed there.

While many people prefer hand-written records, high-tech tools are equally as effective for plenty of brokers. Cell phones are performing amazing tasks and other Personal Data Assistants (PDAs) are indispensable tools for many licensees. If you like this route, Uncle Dave would caution you that if you keep all your information in one place you are exposed to great risk. If you have ever lost a cell phone or had a computer crash or had somebody steal something from you, you know what I mean. But there is a lot to be said for having all that data in the palm of your hand.

It does not make a big difference how you choose to organize, but it is critical to do it somehow. You need to inject quality activities into every day and writing them down lends importance, priority and structure to them. Agents who neglect this responsibility are much more likely to put off or forget the activities which provide lifeblood to the successful pros.

Attending to Pending Transactions

The second step in your three-step plan for productivity is to attend to your pending files. By now, you undoubtedly recognize the importance of referrals, so you cannot afford to disregard the needs of the people who can help you most—past and present clients. Uncle Dave suggests you take out each buyer's file and each listing file, one at a time, and review them every day to be certain there are no loose ends. Make any calls you can to escrow companies, lenders, home inspectors and others that will move those files closer to a payday.

This is the time to make a follow-up call to anybody who has not returned one of your previous calls. You will also observe if you should be seeking price reductions on your listings or modifying tactics for your buyers. Make certain you keep your clients posted so they know you are in control. Some days I could get through this step in a matter of minutes, but other days it took several hours. After you are confident you have moved every file along as far as it can go, it is time to move to step three in your productivity plan.

I find it odd that brokers implement all sorts of fancy programs to locate new business, but then are so cavalier when it comes to attending to their existing clients. Good brokers schedule time for contacting their clients. Then they do it!

It makes sense because the person making the call has control.

For example, if you have an overpriced listing, you have a much better chance of securing a price reduction if you call your seller before they call you. You could say something like this: "Charlie, two other sellers in your neighborhood sold their homes this week but we aren't getting enough action. I have done everything you would expect me to do, but the market is telling us we need to make a price reduction. How much can YOU lower the price?"

Struggling brokers put off calls like that. Instead, they hope the real estate gods will bless them with an ignorant buyer. When that does not happen they are inevitably confronted with a different phone call. It sounds too much like this: "Hey Dave, this is Charlie—you know, that guy who listed his home with you about a month ago. Two of my neighbors sold their homes lately. I haven't heard a word from you and I don't like the way things are going. Why aren't you selling my home?" What an ugly and unnecessary situation!

Seek Out Business

Your office is for working, not social experiences. Your most important responsibility is to generate high-quality leads. There are gobs of ways to do that, including simple things such as calling 3 preferred clients per day or mailing a newsletter to 500 neighbors every month. Let's look at how successful brokers find those precious leads.

If you plant enough seeds, something will grow.

From the Employing Firm

Given your independent contractor status, the managing broker is not obligated to provide you with any business or leads, but many companies have programs in place to help their sales force. Here are the most common ones:

1) Some of them have large national referral networks and they distribute the leads they get from that source.
2) Other possibilities come from their advertising and promotional programs. Any leads from those programs may be available to you.
3) Finally, most companies offer "floor duty" or "up-time." A schedule is followed that allows participating agents to take any incoming calls from newspaper ads, yard signs or walk-in business. Up-time can be fairly productive for agents who develop their phone techniques and take the time to gain familiarity with the inventory.

Any leads received directly from the company should be considered supplemental, not primary. A few extra transactions per year are helpful, but not enough to make a comfortable living. Obviously, when you interview with a firm you should inquire if any leads are provided.

From Your Own Efforts

The bulk of your income needs to come from leads that you generate yourself. The bulk of your income needs to come from leads that you generate yourself. That was not a typing error. Uncle Dave repeated the sentence because it is one of the critical keys that unlock the doors to your success. I suggest you highlight it and write it down. In fact, let's say it out loud together, "The bulk of my income needs to come from leads that I generate myself."

There are several proven ways to do your prospecting. Many successful agents employ a concept called "farming." The theory is if you plant enough seeds, something will grow. There are several types of successful farms and agents commonly employ more than one at the same time. Following are several types of prospecting farms.

The Past Client Farm

The most precious source of business comes from our past clients. Large companies, charities and political groups know the best place to get added revenues is from somebody who is already doing business with them. Your past clients are in that same category for you. We spend gobs of money and effort to find good clients. Surely we should expend a similar amount of resources to retain the people who already like us and are more likely to send us referrals or use us again. The beauty of working with past clients is most of the five steps of a successful sale are already understood, so you can jump to the latter stages right away.

Whenever you meet somebody new, you have to accomplish several goals before they will complete a successful transaction with you. Ordinarily, you have to cover all of these issues:

1. *Why they should buy or sell.*
2. *Why they should work with your company.*
3. *Why they should work with you.*
4. *Why they should buy a particular home or accept a particular offer, and...*
5. *Why they should buy now.*

It is infinitely easier to get business out of somebody who has already had a positive experience working with you. You should

73

begin some sort of marketing campaign to retain these people as soon as they become "past" clients. Your program will include mailing to them, calling them regularly and some sort of occasional socializing.

The Sphere of Influence Farm

Your next best farm is your sphere of influence. In an earlier chapter, Uncle Dave observed this concept as one of the top ten tools you need to have. Now, we can expand on that idea. You will make a list of everybody you know and create ways to stay in touch with them. Some agents have a grading system for these people. If you like this idea, you can label your people as 1's, 2's and 3's, or A's, B's and C's or one-star, two-stars and three-stars, but Uncle Dave likes A, AA and AAA because you might refer to your people by grade sometime and if you tell somebody you consider them to be an "A" client that sounds better than calling them a C or a 3.

The "AAA" clients are the people who are most likely to use the broker themselves or send referrals. This includes close friends, immediate family members, past clients and anyone who is likely to move soon due to changes in family size or work. Good candidates for "AA" ratings include (a) anybody the agent believes might become a good candidate for an AAA rating, (b) an investor who already owns a bunch of rental properties, (c) more distant friends and family members, and (d) people you see somewhat regularly such as your mail carrier, your neighbors and your spouse's family. That leaves everybody else as "A" clients.

If you like the grading system you will put the greatest effort and resources into the people you designated as AAA and the least into the ones who are A's. Over time, you will be surprised because some of the people who you designated as AAA will disappoint you and somebody in you "A" group will send you more business than you expected. Naturally, you can reclassify the people as these things happen.

Once you get 50 people who are deeply committed to sending you referrals, you will have enough business to last you a lifetime.

Do not assume that these people will automatically send you leads. Most of them are engrossed in their own lives and they have no way of realizing how important this is to you. For all they know, you already have a full book of business, so they don't need to get involved.

Common ways to communicate with this group are by mailing monthly newsletters (the best ones are those that you write yourself, but there are services that will write them and personalize them for you so it appears that you write them), send regular mailings (email, or snail mail), make occasional but scheduled phone calls, send them birthday cards (also to their kids) and anniversary cards, and invite them to social activities. Lots of agents send annual customized calendars to the people in their sphere. That is one way the broker can keep his/her name in the eyes and minds of the people in this group. Another successful strategy is to send them large useful magnets with your name and/or picture on them. Nearly everybody turns their refrigerator into a billboard and you will be front and center in their kitchen.

I, the broker, promise to invite you, the insider, to 3 kick-butt parties each year and you promise to send me at least one good referral within the same year. If either of us fails to keep our obligation to the other, the damaged party gets to _ _ _ _!

NOTE: If the reader takes nothing else from this book, I hope you understand the importance of the following promotional concept.

Your goal should be to get 50 people who are deeply committed to sending you referrals. Once you do that, you will have enough business to last you a lifetime. Call them your Top-50 or The Insiders Club or Fabulous 50 or something similar. They can come from your past clients or your sphere.

To begin, you have to find a way to motivate those people to send you referrals. You can invite them to a party and announce your intent, or take them out to dinner and explain why this is so important to you. You might enter into a simple, fun and catchy "contract" which requires them to send you all the referrals they hear of; in exchange, you will invite them (and the other 49 people) to 2-3 parties per year with all the food, drink, music and fun they can handle. Then call them regularly and mail newsletter, birthday cards for them and their kids as well as marketing material, etc. reminding them of their promise. Then enjoy some fantastic parties and an awesome income.

I know of one agent who throws such fabulous parties he has a waiting list for people who want to join his Insiders Club, but he is very firm about limiting the number of people in his club to fifty. By doing that, he keeps the members motivated to fulfill their part of the bargain. His people really do send him referrals because he has made a big production out of it and they don't want to get dropped from the group and miss those parties.

If big parties are not your bag, there are plenty of other options. Uncle Dave rented a luxury box at sporting events quite a few times. It makes a lasting impression and it is a lot of fun. One year, we rented a bus (with a keg in the back) and went white water rafting. Other possibilities include art museums, baseball games, Home and Garden shows, plays, dog races, ski trips, the circus, comedy clubs, rodeo, professional wrestling, bowling, square dancing, roller skating, putt-putt golf, concerts, dinner theaters, and amusement parks. You can rent a movie theater for private showings of first-run movies. Scan your Yellow Pages for other ideas. The possibilities are endless.

Regardless of which activities you select, take lots of pictures or hire somebody to do it for you. Send relevant copies to the members to remind them of how much fun they had. Make up a photo album and use those pictures in your other marketing efforts. Before the activity is over, be sure to give a little speech to thank your guests for coming and then remind them why they are there.

If this seems overwhelming, you can join forces with other brokers within your office to share the expenses and workload. Some entire offices reserve areas in nearby parks with batting cages, baseball fields and other amenities. Then they hold open house-type picnics, hire a live band, and invite all the agents, their families and their past clients to come share in the activities.

Now let me show you how powerful this is. In our area, it is common for a broker to pocket $5,000 or more from the sale of a single median-priced home. If each one of your Top-50 sends you one transaction of that type each year, you'll have a cool quarter-million dollars in annual income. Do you see how important this is?

While other brokers are loitering in the office, wondering how to make a living, you can be among the top-producers. Now you know how to make it fun, too.

The Geographical Farm

> *Ted is among a large group of brokers who hand out pumpkins on Halloween and small yard-sized flags on the Fourth of July.*

In this situation, the licensee chooses a residential neighborhood in which the goal is to become the real estate expert in that area. Usually there are 300 to 1,000 homes in the farm. The licensee learns all the floor plans (if there is a finite number). He/she goes to all the local schools to meet the principals and learns as much as possible about the institutions.

Brokers who employ this concept make a practice of being seen in the neighborhood. It is common for them to walk around the area on Saturdays handing out pot holders or note pads and chatting with anybody who is interested. He/she may put signs on car doors and drive around just to be visible. They look at all new listings in the area so they can talk with authority whenever the opportunity presents itself.

Uncle Dave maintained such a farm for quite a few years. In the beginning I set up a post-card mailing program. Each week for a year I sent 300 people an announcement of some sort. Sometimes it would be about neighborhood news or marketing information. When I obtained a new listing I sent out the cards with a picture of the home on them. When I lowered the price, I sent out another round. The same thing when we accepted an offer and when it actually sold. The post office offers discounts on mailings like this so it cost me about $100 each time I sent out a mailing, which added up to $5,000 for the year. But the commission from one sale covered that. Once my name was established, I was able to cut back on the frequency and enjoyed a steady income from that farm at a very modest cost.

One time I went on a listing appointment in that farm and Mr. Seller told me, "I use to get tired of seeing your marketing cards all the time. Then today my boss notified me I was being transferred. The first thing I did was come home and ask my wife if we had one of your cards around so I could contact you." I got that listing and made about $6,000 off the deal.

One of the best ideas is employed by Rick. He has school-age children and he farms the neighborhood in which his family lives. Every summer he sponsors a community-wide garage sale. About one week prior to the big event he distributes a newsletter in which he lists a couple items offered for sale by each interested family. He also advertises a 300-home garage sale in the local newspaper. On the day of the sale, he sets up welcome signs and makes sure he is very visible. Naturally, he is appreciated throughout the community and everybody knows him well. Oh, by the way, he makes a great living too.

> *If you have the right circumstances you can farm for first-time buyers or investors. It takes a van and a good parking space. Simply have a nice banner painted that you can hang from the side of the van that says:*
>
> ### First-Time Home Buyers' Clinic
> ### Details Here
>
> *Then park it in an area where there are lots of apartments or lots of traffic, somewhere near your office. For investors the sign reads:*
>
> ### Free Investor Seminar Saturday
> ### CALL (123) 456-7890
>
> *Note: Whenever you employ a technique like this, you will be more successful if you do it for at least ten consecutive weeks. People won't usually drop in the first time they see your van there. But the ongoing effort has a residual effect.*

The New Home Farm

Steve and Galen have both done extremely well by working with new home builders. Some of the buyers of new homes had their own homes to sell, so these fellows set up buyout programs and other ways to fulfill that need. When the builders found out how professional these brokers were, the listings rolled in by the bucketful.

The 5x5x5 Farm

Another example of an effective real estate farm is called a "five by five by five." This is a successful technique for any agent who is looking to make a dynamic impression on a seller of a new listing and to pick up some additional clients doing it. Here is how it works.

79

Whenever you take a new listing, you grab a couple dozen brochures or note pads or some other small promotional item and introduce yourself to the immediate neighbors of your seller. First you visit five homes on one side of your listing, then five homes on the other side, and finally five homes across the street. There is nothing magical about the number five and the exact total is not critical either. For example, you could visit one home on one side, twelve or the other side and nine across the street. The point is to go visit with a group of neighbors near your listing.

You knock on the door and say something like, "Hi, my name is Shirley Hoyle and I have just listed the M^{C}Seller home. Whenever I take a new listing, I like to give out brochures to the neighbors, so I have one for you (hands it to them). Oh, by the way, do you know anybody who would like to move into the area?"

Most of the time, they are going to say, "No," but that is fine. You will then ask a follow-up question, "While I am here, do you know anybody else in the area who is thinking of selling?" Obviously, you take the name and number of any leads they give you. But, if the answer is still "no," you simply thank them for their time and tell them you will keep them posted on your efforts and the success with your listing.

> *You have a valid reason to approach homeowners because most of them have a natural curiosity about the homes for sale on their block.*

That is all there is to it. You will be surprised how easy it is to get leads this way. You go back again whenever something new happens. You drop by to announce an upcoming open house or if you lower the price of your listing and when the property has a pending contract and after the transaction has closed. Each time you hand out a small gift and ask if they know of any other people who might be able to use your services. The last time you visit them you also ask if they would like to receive your newsletter. If so, you can obtain their name and number and add them to your sphere of influence.

Now, here is some good news for you. You can employ this idea even if you don't have a listing to promote. All you have to do is ask other agents in your office if you can go out and promote their listings. Most of them will be thrilled to accommodate you. The listing agent simply calls his seller/ client and suggests you are helping market the home. Once you have permission from both the listing broker and the seller you are good to go.

Finally, this is an excellent technique for agents who are somewhat timid or new to an area. You have a valid reason to approach homeowners because most of them have a natural curiosity about the homes for sale on their block. This is one of the best ways I know to approach strangers.

> *If you don't know where your business is going to come from, it is not going to come from anywhere.*

Uncle Dave employed most of the farming systems mentioned. Naturally, I emphasized past clients and sphere of influence farms because the majority of those contacts are by phone or mail so I could reach more of them regularly and with less of a time commitment. I also did well with a geographical farm.

The above examples are common successful farming techniques but you can set up any farm you would like. You could specialize in working with single moms, first-time buyers, athletes, flight attendants, disabled veterans, retired people, mechanics, widows, accountants, cowgirls or all the people who work in a high-rise office building near your home. All you have to do is seek out that business and constantly remind those people that you want to work with them.

From Special Promotions

There are additional effective ways to generate your own business. One of the most common ones is to hold open houses. Another is to write ads for the local newspapers. And of course, there is the fabulous Internet.

Hold Open Houses

By now, you should realize you do not need to be the listing broker of the home to promote it. You just need to secure permission from the listing agent and the owner. There are a lot of people who will be happy to accommodate you.

Nearly any veteran broker can tell you how to hold a home open, but let me remind you there is nothing stopping you from calling members of your Fabulous 50 or knocking on 5x5x5 doors ahead of time to announce your plans and invite them to come to the open house. The objective is to show people you are working. Plant those seeds.

You should also realize that you owe it to the listing broker and the seller to make every reasonable effort to sell that home if a buyer shows up and expresses interest in it. Once in a while that will actually happen. If you do accomplish that, you will receive the commission which was earmarked for the selling broker. Yahoo! The harder you work, the luckier you get.

Once you have determined the buyer is not going to buy the subject property, you are free to ask them if you can show them additional homes. You will have a couple alternatives in mind because you did your homework in advance.

Newspaper Ads

Prior to the Internet, this was a very common way to sell homes. Interestingly, ads are still effective because relatively few agents employ the technique so those who run effective ads have a good shot at the buyers who shop for homes and information this way.

The trick to this concept is to write good ads and develop good telephone techniques. It is a waste of precious marketing dollars to run ads and then lack the knowledge to handle the incoming calls. Your broker will teach you how to handle this responsibility. You will have to practice what to say, but it gets easier with a little effort. Once again you can advertise another broker's listing, with permission.

Internet

One expert told me that 80% of the buyers spend time online looking at homes before they align themselves with a broker. There are all sorts of ways to use this dynamic tool for effective marketing. You can promote yourself on those social personal networks. Hundreds of brokers use MySpace and similar sites for this purpose. You can start a blog and invite your friends, families, clients and others to participate. You can set up mass email lists to search for new buyers or sellers. And of course you can establish a personal Web site.

One of the more effective ways to generate business from the Internet is from Craigslist. This has become so popular you can pick up buyers for your listings and contact other sellers to discover which ones might be thinking of hiring a broker. Uncle Dave uses Craigslist to find tenants for rental properties. It works well. Here's what to include:

A well-written ad accomplishes these things, usually in order:

Attention
Interest
Desire
Action

THIS LARGE FAMILY DREAM-HOME is amazingly cozy. 5 beds 4 baths Cherokee Vistas. Cul de Sac. Park-like yard and close to schools. Priced right! Trade-in program available. Call Uncle Dave at 3:00 in the morning.

Do you see the four steps within the ad?

Specialties

There are numerous less common ways to generate your own business. Their appeal is not broad enough to warrant in-depth discussion, but let's look at a few of them with some simple explanations.

- Mall shows - I have picked up 20 leads in a weekend by renting a table at home and garden shows
- Hand out pencils on the corner - for fun and variety
- Bus benches - great way to build name recognition in a specific neighborhood
- Put your name on grocery carts - same as above
- Host your own radio shows - takes a lot of effort but creates credibility
- Host seminars - great for first-time buyers or entry-level investors
- Bank-owned properties - A little difficult to get your foot in the door but a good source of repeat business
- TV and radio ads - expensive but very powerful

- Mail fliers into areas with lots of apartment buildings - tenants become first-time buyers
- Align with large corporations - they transfer buyers in and sellers out
- Work with senior-housing facilities - they help

JOKE TIME - Three passengers were on a small plane that was about to crash. One passenger was a 10-year-old girl. The other two were Realtors returning from an awards banquet where one Realtor was recognized for being the Smartest Realtor, and the other one took first place in the category of being the Kindest Realtor. There were only two parachutes on the plane so the smartest Realtor quickly grabbed one of them and said, "A lot of people need me, so I get one of these" and he jumped out of the plane. The kindest Realtor turned to the girl and said, "You are young and have so much to look forward to. Please take the last parachute." The young girl responded, "Oh, don't worry, we both get a parachute. The smartest Realtor just grabbed my backpack."

As I close out this chapter I am mindful of how unfortunate it is that people get a license and then struggle because they don't know what to do. The real estate business is relatively easy to figure out. All you have to do is approach the day as if it is a simple game. There are three periods in the game: (1) first, organize your day; (2) then take care of your current and past clients; and (3) contact people and ask for business. IT IS THAT SIMPLE! If you do that, you will make a good living, but if you do not do that, you will probably fail. Now you know some good ways to do it.

Finally, before you decide what marketing plans are best for you, you should have a lengthy discussion with your broker, other agents and your spouse to fine-tune a system that you can embrace. Your loving uncle cautions you to be realistic in your undertakings. It is much better to strive for attainable successes than fizzle out because of wild exuberance; for example, if you are planning on creating a calling list, it would be within reach to contact 100 people you know within a month, but it would be nearly impossible to call 5,000 people whom you do not know.

The best thing you can do is identify the people who can help you the most and let them know how much you need them. Consistent referrals from that group can overcome all your other weaknesses. The business is out there but it has no incentive to come find you. So, go get it.

This true story ought to show you just how valuable good systems can be.

Uncle Dave's True Story #7: I Do, I Do, and I Do, Too

One evening I received a call from Mike and Becky, who saw my personal phone number on a yard sign at one of my listings. I did not know them at the time. After dispensing with the usual procedures they bought the home without a hint of drama, but that situation would soon change.

About six months later, Becky called and announced that Mike moved out. A few months later the divorce was final and they wanted to sell the home. I met each of them separately and took the listing.

After their home sold, Becky moved into an apartment with her mother, but Mike was ready to buy a townhome, so I quickly found him a nice one and he eagerly moved in, ready to fulfill all the dreams of a new bachelor.

A couple more months passed by and Becky called me to see about buying a home near the school of her children. Naturally, I was happy to help her. Before long the mission was accomplished. Then her mother moved in with her and the grandkids.

Another few months passed before I got the next call. I was surprised to learn that Mike had a new bride. Fortunately for me, she didn't really want to live townhome-style. I listed and sold Mike's place, and you know the pattern.

It only took a few weeks to locate their new home, nearer her work.

Then Becky called again. She also remarried. Her new husband was a nice fellow who moved in with Becky and her mother, but by then, Grandma wanted a home of her own. I found her one just a few blocks away.

That adds up to seven transactions in a two-year period. What a superfantabulous chain!

Think about it. What did you learn?

Hint: Think about the early part of this chapter and as a more humorous point, think about attorneys.

Go to page 220 for your Instant Experience.

Chapter 8 – UNCLE DAVE'S SHORTS
or
Quick Hits

This chapter is comprised of short topics that are useful to know, but do not require lengthy explanations. I put it in this part of the book because the next two chapters are lengthy and require a little deeper thought. We can consider this section to be "the calm before the storm." There is no particular order to the topics, so just read, ponder, and enjoy.

A Priority Check

New brokers will do well to keep their lives in balance.

Ironically, excessive responsibility is a shortcoming for some licensees. Tragically, this over-commitment to their work amounts to negligence of their families and themselves. They think all their extra effort indicates a strong sense of responsibility, but I would suggest the opposite is true. I never did consider it "responsible" to live a life like that.

People who sacrifice their families and personal life for more dollars than they need have a priority problem. Far too often, that lack of balance in their lives leads to burn-out. Uncle Dave believes you will be better off if you invest plenty of your time on the things that bring other forms of wealth into your life.

Getting Down

Answer this simple question: If a buyer puts twenty thousand dollars down on a one-hundred thousand dollar townhome, what percentage is she financing? The answer is that it depends on who you ask. From the lender's perspective the buyer is financing 80% or $80,000. But from the buyer's perspective, every property is 100% financed.

The buyer's money has to come from somewhere. Usually a lender kicks in a loan for a high percentage of the purchase price, and the buyer brings in the remainder, but from where? If that money was in a savings account, the buyer is no longer enjoying interest on that money; hence, there is an interest expense for it. If the money comes from a mutual fund, the buyer forfeits the "opportunity cost" of those monies. If Mom and Dad kick in the down payment for the buyer, they are losing the money they could have earned by placing that money somewhere else. Therefore, the entire purchase price has some sort of interest cost and that means all buyers finance 100% of the purchase price, in one way or the other.

Ants and Anteaters

You are probably a nice person, but there are times when that splendid quality will work against you. If you think about it, it makes sense. Most any good trait can work against us. For example, people who trust others are more likely to leave their cars unlocked and then become the victims of thieves. If you are generous, there are those who will be glad to take advantage of you. There are bosses who exploit hard workers. Nice people, like you, have problems too. When it comes to day-to-day life in the real estate world, Uncle Dave would like to tell you that all your associates will play nice like you do, but that would just set you up for disappointment.

The truth is there are plenty of nice people in the industry who act like ants, working together for a common cause. Each one knows his or her role within the colony and sticks to that job. This cooperative spirit can lead to communities with millions of citizens. But, there are also a few anteaters around, and those sharp-clawed, long-tongued predators also survive, usually by feasting on ants. Customers, clients, competitors, co-workers and managing brokers can take either form.

Nice brokers are especially vulnerable when they don't press for the signature. Since most phases of the transaction must be in writing to be enforceable, it is very risky to trust that your prospective seller will sign the listing agreement tomorrow. If you believe your clients will appreciate your low-key style so you let them "think about it" overnight, an anteater may come out of the shadows and persuade them to employ him instead.

It is nice to be nice, and it is foolish to be foolish. Why give your competitors extra opportunities to slurp you up? If you give anteaters extra chances, some of them will do almost anything to capture YOUR BUSINESS, usually when you least expect it.

Look Who's Wearing the Pants

Some marriages struggle when the woman enters our profession and does especially well. That is because the husband feels threatened by her success. He may feel neglected or inadequate if she begins making more money than he does. He may not like the fact she has evening appointments or that she dresses up when she leaves the house or spends so much time away. If this happens to you, Uncle Dave suggests you go get counseling right away. If you can't come to grips with this situation early on, it has the potential to destroy your relationship.

Overcoming Dry Spells

One of the primary goals of every licensee is to keep those commissions coming in on a regular and dependable basis. There are ways to swing the system in your favor, but sooner or later, it happens to all of us. Two or three transactions fall apart, all at the same time. We are still prospecting for new business, but hot and immediate leads are elusive. Your listings seem priced right, but no buyers are taking the bait. You wonder if you have irritated a witch or something.

When this happens to you, there are several things you can do to get out of your own personal funk. First, get out a motivational tape or book and look for some inspiration. Second, go back to the basics. Review your schedule to determine if you are spending your time wisely. Third, remember that in baseball four singles are just as good as a home run. Look for some small success that will help you get to first base and regain your momentum. Fourth, somehow the universe seems programmed to send us business whenever we would rather not be disturbed, so distract yourself with one of those extracurricular activities you've been meaning to do. For instance, go on a spontaneous weekend getaway or paint the trim on your home.

Another inspirational technique is to go on a couple of appointments with co-workers. The public loves it when extra people show interest in them and you will probably learn something new. Finally, it may be time to put things in perspective. Serve meals at a homeless shelter. Take a senior to the grocery store or visit a veteran. When you are reminded how good you have it, a little humility may be good for you.

Goals

Some agents swear by the power of goals, but not Uncle Dave. After a few years, I stopped setting goals for myself. The way I see it, Realtors average about ten transactions per year. If I set my goal to complete 40 transactions and then completed 30 of them, it is ridiculous to feel disappointment while accomplishing three times the national average. Eventually, I concluded I was making a pleasant living and serving people well and that was good enough.

I have seen people burn out by chasing goals. As soon as the agent accomplishes the current goal, the bar is raised, and he or she is always under pressure to fulfill higher expectations. That ain't for this uncle.

Who Prepares Your Tax Return?

Uncle Dave suggests you align yourself with a CPA who does not have other real estate agents as clients, which usually means one of the younger ones. These professionals are good sources for referrals. They know people who hate paying excessive taxes and those people make good first-time buyers and entry-level investors.

Find the Oxymoron in this Paragraph

As you wind your way through the business, you will read books, attend seminars and meet all sorts of interesting people. Whenever you meet somebody who has inspired you in some way it is fine to learn from them, but do not attempt to be just like them. You will be much more successful if you strive to become a better version of you, not a better somebody else. Uncle Dave knows gobs of successful brokers and they are all unique. Uncle Dave suggests you strive to be a nonconformist, just like them. That will make you more interesting.

Who Really Pays Commissions?

Most seasoned agents tell us that sellers usually pay our commissions, but Uncle Dave says otherwise. Oh sure, the money comes off the seller's ledger, but it is the buyer's money. Once the contract is executed, it is the buyer who has to round up the money to pay for everything. The funds are distributed to pay all the expenses of the closing, including commissions; then, the seller keeps whatever is left over. If the buyer paid everybody directly, it would be clearer.

The current system offers two benefits to taking the expenses from the seller's side of the ledger. First it reduces the buyer's out-of-pocket costs. If the home price was $200,000 and the buyer paid an extra $10,000 (5%) to the brokers, the lender would make the loan based on the purchase price, not the total cost. Thus, the loan would be much lower and the out-of-pocket amount for the buyer would be much higher.

Second, the brokers also benefit by taking their fee right off the top rather than as an add-on. In the previous example, the broker's fee was $10,000, but if the same broker charged 5% of $210,000 he or she would get $10,500, which is an extra five hundred bucks.

So, the benefits of taking the money from the seller obscure a simple truth. The buyer pays for everything, including commissions. Share this concept with the old pros in your office and they will think you are a deep thinker.

From Apathy to Passion

When it comes to succeeding in real estate sales, there are various degrees of commitment. Some people are totally apathetic, others are willing, there are those who are enthusiastic and some are genuinely motivated. Motivation is powerful.

But as powerful as motivation is, it pales compared to its big brother, passion. Passion is a rare commodity. Some people never feel truly passionate about anything. Only a very few people have a true passion for our business. Uncle Dave has always been one of those select few. I hope you will join me.

A Matter of Perspective

Things will go against you from time to time. Interest rates go up, markets decline, clients lie to you or change their minds. Naturally, you can adjust to your own mistakes but you cannot do much to combat external forces, except to adjust your perspective.

One year we were bemoaning the local market when a new fellow, named Ken, joined our office. He came from Detroit, which was experiencing an even tougher market. Ken thought we had it easy. That kind of perspective served him well. In spite of the fact that he did not know any of our neighborhoods or local matters, he started making money right under our noses. His very first listing was a sign of things to come. He spent several hours with a motivated seller. By the time he left their home, he had successfully persuaded them to offer a very aggressive price. Then he sealed the deal for his client by encouraging them to accept terms that other sellers could not or would not ordinarily consider.

When he introduced his listing at our sales meeting, I immediately knew the perfect investor-buyer for the home. The terms were what made it work. A few weeks later we completed the closing and Ken's seller was moving on while other sellers in the neighborhood watched weeds overtake the for sale signs in their yards. That was twenty years ago and Ken is still going strong.

When things seem difficult, remember that other people have it worse than you do and adjust your perspective.

Are You Planning on Getting a License Just to Save Commissions on Your Own Transactions?

This usually is not a good idea unless you are an investor who intends to get in and out of multiple transactions.

When you are the buyer of a home in which you intend to

live, you can sometimes lower the purchase price and waive the commission you would have received, but that technique has some side problems. For example, when you lower the purchase price, it usually lowers the maximum loan amount you can obtain. Next, under some conditions, any savings you enjoy may result in higher taxes when you resell the property. Also, your broker expects you to put a few coins in his or her cash register from time to time, so you will have to attend to that loose end. Finally, if you take the commission rather than the price savings, the income might make it easier for you to qualify for future loans.

When you are a seller and try to take a higher sales price rather than the commissions, you have similar problems. Once again, you still have an obligation to pay your broker his or her share. Next, you do not get to report the commission as income, which could help you to qualify for future loans. However, there is one benefit to foregoing the commission charge and taking the money as in a higher sales price. Some or all of the "profit" could be free of taxes while commission checks are usually subject to income taxes.

When we review the small savings and weigh the costs and time necessary to obtain a license for these purposes, the net gain is minimal. Furthermore, it may be a long time before you can repeat the process.

If you are an investor who expects to be involved in multiple transactions, the license will be more valuable to you.

Seek Out Experts

The previous paragraph screams for this follow-up topic. If you read something you like in this book or elsewhere, it is your responsibility to verify whether the information applies to you. In addition, there are occasions when a customer asks you a question that requires the counsel of experts before you respond, so you need immediate access to a wide range of useful experts.

Peaks and Valleys

A common problem for new agents is the inevitable peaks and valleys which are visited upon us, especially early in our careers. The most common cause of this unpleasant experience is a neglect of prospecting. The pattern is predictable. We get three or four transactions in the fire all at once. Then we are so busy attending to the details we run out of time, and we put off prospecting.

> *JOKE TIME - Two tired and struggling brokers went to lunch to discuss their woes. When the waitress approached them to take their order she heard them complaining so she asked, "How are you fellows today?" One customer said to her, "We're in real estate and we're not making enough money." Trying to replace the tension with a little humor the cheerful waitress smiled and asked, "So which one of you is the broker broker?" Without missing a beat, the first customer said, "I am, because I have been out of commission for four months." Not to be outdone, the other broker quipped, "Ah, that's nothing; I have been listless for the entire year."*

A few weeks later, after all those deals close, we realize we have no new transactions in the pipeline. The next month looks bleak so a minor panic sets in. We know we have neglected our prospecting so we try to make up for lost ground. We work hard, make extra calls and chase every lead with vigor.

Eventually, we find some people we can help. Then, reality sets in. Our new listings may take a while to sell. Our new buyers may not find their new home in a timely manner; any potential closing date is 4-12 weeks away. The next month, our bills roll around and the wallet is thin.

Then a new level takes over. Those new transactions go under contract, all at the same time. Naturally, all that new business is followed by chaos as we strive to attend to the details needed to complete them successfully, and we are right back where we started.

The effect of peaks and valleys can be flattened out with consistent prospecting. If you find yourself so busy you are tempted to put off this important activity, your priorities are out of whack. The correct solution to your short-term dilemma is to hire temporary help to attend to some of the details. You can hire a runner to deliver contracts for you. One of your friends in the office might be able to attend your closings. You can delegate detail work to secretaries and assistants. Your broker is supposed to be a "managing" broker. It is okay to ask for help when you are swamped. Then get back to your consistent prospecting.

Local Trends

Some markets tend to ebb and flow like a tide; others are remarkably stable. When prices are heading up, it is more difficult to land new listings. Some sellers get cocky and try to sell their homes themselves. Others instinctively realize they are in a stronger bargaining position, so they are inclined to seek agents who will work for less. Sometimes there will be multiple offers on the new listings.

In that same environment, the buyers will be jumping into your lap like salmon heading upstream because they need you more than the sellers do. Agents who have built up their client bases are poised for some remarkable success. That is also the time that new agents emerge to see if they can get in on the glory.

The challenge in a market like that is to keep prospecting. It may seem like you have to do all the running you can just to keep up, but that is exactly what you want to exploit. Uncle Dave suggests you hire some temporary help to work some of your leads for a cut of the deal. When the spawning season is over you can cut back if you want to, but you must fill your boat while the opportunity is there.

When the market is in a decline, fear is the driving emotion. Buyers don't want to take on the risk of losing money and many owners have a difficult time lowering their prices below the once-higher values. But sellers need you then, so they will be easier to deal with than they are in an appreciating market. Any buyers you can find equal money in the bank because they will have plenty of inventory from which to choose, and some seller will give them a good deal, making you look like the hero.

So, in an increasing market new listings are gold and in a declining market the buyers will bring you the easiest and quickest paydays. If you are in one of those always-flat markets, count your blessing because everybody needs you.

If your market is among the less stable ones, it would serve you to anticipate the circumstances a year or so down the road and prepare accordingly. The best book I know of on the topic is called *Financial Freedom in Five Years*, written by Sean Moudry. He does a great job of instructing readers on how to determine the direction of their market.

Broader Trends

The older baby boomers are starting to retire now. Their life expectancy is about 77 years. The last baby boomers will retire in about 10-15 years. That means a trainload of seniors are just over the horizon and they are headed our way. These facts open up several opportunities for licensees.

There are agents who specialize in working with seniors and the future looks bright for those brokers. Lots of the empty nesters will be looking to move into smaller homes with fewer stairs and postage stamp-size yards. Others will move to more affordable communities in small towns or out in the country.

Fantastic retirement communities are popping up all over the place. Many of these projects are more like exciting dormitories than the tired versions of similar facilities from days gone by. Residents enjoy the company of like-minded friends. Activity coordinators organize interesting events right in the community, and shuttle buses are utilized to visit local events, grocery stores and other appropriate places.

Another trend of this group is found in second-home markets. There are many communities in the warmer areas that attract these folks, especially in the winter. Lavish golf courses are surrounded by mobile-home communities, with occupants spending more time scurrying around in electric carts than they do in their automobiles. Seniors discover exciting new friendships and look forward to returning year after year.

The well-to-do seniors are not the only ones who make changes. A compassionate society is constantly seeking ways to build or provide affordable housing for the ones with fewer financial options.

As for the rest of society, the cost of heating and cooling our homes continues to rise, which will send millions of us into energy-efficient alternatives. The same high energy costs will encourage county and state officials to revitalize their inner cities, where housing is cheaper and the infrastructure is in place. I would expect old apartment buildings to be converted into condominiums and older office buildings and warehouses to be upgraded into modern apartments.

Energy costs may lead to more four-day work weeks, leaving more time off for workers. As citizens gain more personal time, they will be inclined to travel so time-shares and vacation homes may enjoy new demand.

All the new automobiles inspire imagination. As vehicles get smaller, new homes will be built with new purposes for our garages. Recharging stations for powerful batteries may be the norm. Some of us might hook up to our natural gas lines to fuel our cars.

There are still other issues in the mix. If interest rates go up or lenders make it harder for people to obtain loans, we just might find people staying in their homes longer, reducing some of the resale opportunities for agents.

And then there is that little "fad" called the Internet. As the public gets better access to information, some people will find ways to circumvent the role of the real estate agent. It will work out for them sometimes and cause serious problems for them on other occasions.

And finally, there is the illegal immigration issue. If these people are granted immunity, there will be a large pool of new buyers and upward pressure on prices. On the other hand, if they are sent home, we will have vacancies everywhere and I would expect declining prices and a long, long, long weak market, especially in the lower price ranges.

Selling Out

By now you know how important prospecting is. In spite of that fact, many agents dread it. In America there are entrepreneurs who capitalize on situations like that. So, certain companies hire people to make phone calls and generate "leads." The telemarketing company then makes one more call—to you. They offer to sell you a territory. You get all the leads in a certain area in exchange for a sign-up fee and a piece of the action. I never did buy a territory but plenty of agents have.

I have never heard of an agent who renewed his or her contract. The problem is the telemarketing people don't really know the difference between a hot lead and a phone number on a bathroom stall. I am sure some brokers have made a dollar or two off leads generated this way, but most veteran agents will tell you that nothing works like the basics. Uncle Dave suggests you resist the temptation to buy territories from telemarketers.

Setting Appointments

Certain businesses have learned to set their delivery times or appointments within general time windows rather than at specific times. Uncle Dave suggests you incorporate the same idea. I usually suggested, "Let's meet 'sevenish' (rather than at 7:00)." I went on to explain, "That way, if either of us runs into a minor snag, we don't have to feel like we are late." That technique is a good stress reducer. Then try to be punctual anyway.

Playing Fair

When it comes to the Fair Housing Laws, you are about to join an industry obsessed. From mandatory classes to office sales meetings to training courses to back room conversations at the water cooler, everybody is walking on eggshells. Some forms of discrimination are justified and sometimes it is illegal.

You are discriminating if you elect to specialize in selling high-end homes but don't work with investors. If you sell ranches, you may not have any interest in selling homes in the city. Or, you might own a rental property and refuse to rent it to used-car salesmen.

In the last example, the situation becomes more interesting if the used-car salesman happens to be an African-American. That is because he is a member of a protected class of people (based on color or national origin) who is guaranteed equal treatment in housing matters. However, it would still be okay to turn down the salesman, because used-car salesmen are not a protected class and that is the reason he was denied the apartment.

So, we can recognize that discrimination is going on all the time. Sometimes, it is okay and sometimes it is not. You will hear a lot more about this topic as you work your way through real estate school, Realtor courses and your own office policies.

Before you proceed in your quest to obtain a license, Uncle Dave suggests you think about this: If you have personal reasons that you will have to "be careful" when it comes to dealing with people of the protected classes, then our business is not well suited to you. If you achieve any level of success, you will meet a wide variety of people, and there will be plenty of chances for you to get into trouble. You might as well save yourself a bunch of aggravation.

Speaking of people in "protected classes," let me introduce you to Louie.

Uncle Dave's True Story #8: In the Eye of the Beholder

One of my more interesting residential transactions began the day I received a referral from a past client who was a city employee. She told me that Louie, who happened to be blind, ran a concession stand in an office building in which they both worked. He wanted to buy a condominium close to his work, so I agreed to help him. "Showing" property to Louie presented some interesting challenges for Uncle Dave. For one thing, I made certain I described the properties in much better detail than I ordinarily would have done. We "looked" at about ten properties before he found the one he wanted.

Interestingly, he settled on one that looked horrible to most sighted people because it was dark and needed paint and cleaning, but that did not matter to Louie as much as the convenient access to his work. Naturally, I was concerned about his choice because I did not know how he might respond if somebody later told him he bought an ugly duckling. I told him of my apprehension and he agreed to invite a couple of his friends to come inspect it with us.

They confirmed my findings, but the great access to his work trumped everything else. His friends enthusiastically helped him clean it up and he lived there for many years. Eventually, he took a similar position in another big city, and I helped him resell his property. I never heard from him again.

Think about it. What did you learn?

Hint: Consider Fair Housing laws and seeking experts.

Go to page 220 for your Instant Experience.

Chapter 9 – GROWING YOUR MIDDLE
or
Budgeting for Success

That dynamic third leg of the Stool of Knowledge sure has a lot to offer, but the best is yet to come. The next two chapters can change your life. Are you ready?

One of my favorite agents is Rocky. We frequently went to lunch to brainstorm our plans. He was never Salesman of the Year, but he was consistently a Top-5 kind of guy. Rocky had a great way of budgeting that enabled him to lead a very fulfilling life. It is a fantastic concept and Uncle Dave highly recommends it.

I can still see Rocky's hand gestures in my mind's eye, as he would explain how he treated his income. As he swiped his hands through the air in a horizontal fashion, he explained that all of his money was destined to go into one of three categories: the top, the bottom or the middle.

The top portion was for all the money he absolutely needed to cover household expenses. First, he always made certain he had enough money in savings to cover six months of expenses, just in case he had a slow month or two. He called that account his "sleeping money." Then he allowed for other expenses. Those include mortgage payments, groceries, all of his income taxes, insurance and the like. Rocky drove a nice car, he went on respectable vacations and he lived well, but he was never foolish with any of the money that he earmarked for the top section of his budget.

The bottom portion was for the funds he needed to cover his business expenses. Once again, he was prudent. Rocky knew he had to invest in himself so he developed excellent marketing programs, including publishing his own newspaper and circulating it in a nice upper-middle class neighborhood, but he rarely wasted money on silly fads.

Rocky considered it his sacred obligation to fully fund the upper and lower portions of his budget before any money would be spent or invested on anything else, which was "the middle."

The middle was a powerful source of inspiration for Rocky. It was clearly his self-proclaimed reward. The money that went into the middle was "his money." It was for funding his retirement or to enhance his lifestyle, and he did plenty of both. One year the middle had grown sufficiently, so he bought a lakefront home for summer vacations and other getaways.

Rocky's clear vision of how to distribute his funds enabled him to retire at a young age; but just when he was ready to kick back he had a curve ball thrown at him. His son grew up and wanted to join my friend in the business. That flattered and inspired Rocky to rethink his long-term plans. After all those years of planning and obsessing for retirement, he fell upon an opportunity he liked even more—working with Jason. Now they are both doing very well. That happens quite a bit in this business. There are plenty of second-generation brokers.

Rocky always knew his objective was to grow the middle, so he made that the focus of his professional life—a very successful and blessed life, indeed.

Developing Your Own Financial System

When we review Rocky's method, we quickly realize it is like many other ideas within the industry and within this book: It is a lot easier to say than do. Chances are, you would love to implement a system like Rocky's, but your circumstances are very challenging. Still, if you don't figure out a way to get on top of your finances, you are asking for trouble for reasons discussed earlier.

Avoiding stress is one very important reason to get your finances under control, but there is an even greater reason to do this. It has to do with "passive income." Passive income is money that comes to you on a regular basis, whether you work or not.

My friend, Rocky, said it very well when he suggested, "You are financially secure when your passive income exceeds your fixed monthly expenses." Naturally, I wholeheartedly agree with him. When it comes to family finances there is no better feeling than knowing the bills are covered even if you have a long string of bad luck or never even work again. WHEW!

A great way to build your passive income comes from your better months. When you do especially well, I urge you to restrain yourself. Do not run out to buy jewelry, fancy vacations or new automobiles. Instead, you should stash away the equivalent of several months' expenses before you entertain any frivolous spending.

After several more months, if you have added to your savings and still have transactions in the works, it is finally time to celebrate. I suggest you go get an ice cream cone.

You are financially secure when your passive income exceeds your fixed monthly expenses.

We will discuss a more aggressive way to grow your passive income in the next chapter, but first I have some very special information to share with you.

I am trying to explain something much more important than "how to make money." I am trying to demonstrate exactly what to do with it. With that objective in mind, this entire chapter (and the next one) can be a life-changer for you. I hope you will take your time and commit to the ideas herein.

I am going to share a very simple three-step blueprint which will solve your financial problems forever. If you are already financially disciplined, you should read the chapter anyway. There is still plenty of useful information for you. If you have never really committed to financial discipline, this is your opportunity to use your new career as a springboard to long-term financial independence.

My formula is a variation of several others which I have observed over the years, but it is different because it is very simple and it is especially well suited to real estate professionals like you. With that said, there are three basic steps to help you attain wealth over time. It is my pleasure to share them with you.

Step One – HATE DEBT

Have you ever known anybody who suffered with cancer? Everything they do is filtered through their illness. That damn disease screws up everything in their lives and usually the lives of other people too.

Debt, and the inevitable interest hell that tags along with it, are a cancer to your financial body. Debt diminishes your potential. It steals away new opportunities. It causes stress. It distracts you. The good news is there are some very easy treatments.

If you can't pay cash, you can't afford it.

In order to attain true financial freedom, you must confront debt and interest with the same zeal that cancer patients attack their disease. Every purchase you make needs to be filtered through a couple of hard questions: "Do I really need this?" and "Can I pay cash for it?" If the answer to either of those questions is "No," you should recognize the item as a symptom of your financial disease.

Uncle Dave recommends you adopt the following philosophy: "If you can't pay cash, you can't afford it." If you live by that rule, you will reserve your cash for the few things that really matter rather than throw it at all the dumb things that do not.

At first, the idea seems a little daunting but I assure you it is fairly easy. I know lots of people who live this way, but I also know plenty of people who struggle with their finances because their paychecks are always spent before they receive them. Which group are you in?

It has been eighteen years since Uncle Dave financed anything, unless I could get somebody else to pay the debt for me (like a rental property). I remember the day I made my final car payment. That was a great new beginning. About 10 years later, I had enough money to last me a lifetime. All of that is possible by adopting the first step in my simple financial system: HATE DEBT. Hate it with all of your being. Do not let it invade and diminish your life for one more day. Remember to constantly ask yourself, "Do I really need this?" and "Can I pay cash for it?"

If you already have a package of debt you should begin a list of your creditors (do not include your home mortgage or landlord in this group). Prioritize them according to which ones you can pay off first or which ones have the highest interest rate. Start paying 10-20% extra to the number one item on your list and nothing extra to any others. Once you get the first item paid off, reward yourself in some modest way, like going out for another ice cream cone (well, this chapter is called "Growing Your Middle," isn't it?) Then reprioritize your list, and do the same thing with a new item on top.

Do not allow yourself to accumulate any new debt. If your car has become a clunker, do not run out and buy a new one unless you can pay cash. Instead, you should have a small amount of breathing room by paying off that first item so pay about half that monthly amount into a new savings account which is strictly earmarked to upgrade your transportation. Eventually, you will have enough money to pay cash for a cheap-but-reliable car that will get you by for a couple of years.

Depending on your circumstances, it may take you a few

years to dig your way completely out of your financial hole, but in the grand scheme of life, that is a relatively short period of time. You will quickly become proud of your progress and truly hate the debt that is responsible for all of your current sacrifices.

Step 2 – SAVE CONSISTENTLY

Albert Einstein is sometimes credited (wrongly) with identifying compound interest as the eighth wonder of the world. He is not the only one who has observed the power of saving and compounding. There is a charming book about the subject titled *The Richest Man in Babylon*. It should be required reading for high school students. Its lessons about accumulating unearned income are priceless. I certainly recommend it. Another great book that covers the importance of consistent saving is *The Wealthy Barber*. I have purchased dozens of them just to give away.

> *How much is $100 per month worth? Suppose you inherit $100 per month for ten years. How much is that worth in a lump sum? The answer is coming up!*

Hating and eliminating debt is not enough. In order to grow your passive income you must find some money to save and save consistently. Ironically, the best way to do that is to take on a brand new creditor…YOU! You should be the most important beneficiary of your money, more important than the mortgage company, more important than the utility company, more important than everybody. It is time for you to pay yourself first. If there is not enough money to buy everything you want, make some simple adjustments: For example, stop paying the convenience store for latte. It is better to make Seven-Eleven get by without your $4 than it is for you to live without financial security.

> *If you can save one hundred dollars per month for 10 years, and if you can earn 7% annual interest on your savings, you will accumulate enough money to pull out $100 per month for all the rest of eternity. Wow! (If you don't know where you can get 7%, give me a call. I know some investors who would love to talk with you.)*

Uncle Dave suggests you IMMEDIATELY begin saving $100 per month and give that money to you - in a brand-new savings account. This money is not for a new car, or emergencies, or a fancy vacation, or medical bills or anything except your future. You are going to use it to create passive income, income you can live on whether you work or not. It is sacred money, waiting for the right opportunity to be invested.

Each time you knock a creditor off your list YOU GET A RAISE. You can instantly increase the amount you pay to YOUR savings account by half of the amount you have been paying that creditor. The other half of the money is for a modest increase in your standard of living. Keep doing that until you pay off all your debts and then consistently save 10% of everything you make after that. Then you can live on whatever is left over.

If you are like many others, you believe it is impossible to save that much money because you already need everything you make just to get by. But you are mistaken. I realize that seems awfully arrogant of me but please follow the reasoning. There are plenty of people getting by on 90% of what you make. All you have to do is live like they do. Your problem is not that you earn too little. Your problem is that you spend too much and on the wrong things. You are already making enough money to do this. All you have to do is discover where you are spending money now that you could redirect for this purpose. Here is how to do it.

A while back, I wrote an article about the 10 worst things we spend our money on. The full details are not necessary here, but the categories are mentioned below, along with a couple of simple comments. As you read through the list, look for areas where you can reduce some of your expenses. By redirecting those funds you can begin to save $100/month consistently.

1. Conveniences, such as going out to dinner too often, buying items from vending machines or nearly any purchases at convenience stores (imagine that!).
2. Gambling – lottery tickets are the very worst. Trips to casinos.
3. Adult indulgences like alcohol, tobacco, drugs, season tickets to sporting events, lattes at upscale coffee shops, jewelry, sporting toys, upgraded cable TV packages, health club memberships, too many pets, land line telephones if you already have a cell phone.
4. Misbehavior in the eyes of the law – includes traffic tickets, fines, court systems.
5. Financial institutions: ATM fees, bounced check charges, excessive interest on credit cards, closing costs from repeatedly refinancing your home.
6. Most insurance: whole life insurance, extended warranties, low deductibles on auto or hazard insurance that cause higher premiums, excessive insurance for older cars.
7. Renting and leasing nearly anything (e.g., cars), except for one-time needs.
8. Interest, unless you can get somebody else to pay it for you, like interest on a loan for a rental property. If you have auto loans or credit cards you are probably paying at least $100/month in interest, which could be coming to you.
9. Depreciating assets – especially buying new cars and other big-ticket items.
10. Taxes – especially income taxes and death taxes.

Practically everybody, including me, can find some savable money within that group. That is valuable money you can start paying yourself right now. You will soon be investing that money for passive income. Sit down with a friend or loved one and discuss these things. Once you have identified the areas you can improve, write them down and mean it. This dynamic plan is of no use if you don't take action, so go to the bank and open a new savings account RIGHT NOW! Deposit that first $100. Write down what you are doing and why you have decided to change your spending habits and saving philosophy. Keep that note with you or on your refrigerator for at least 3 months, or until it becomes a way of life.

> *If Christopher Columbus had deposited one cent in a bank, and it earned 6% annual interest, that lonely penny would now be worth a remarkable 100 billion dollars and growing by $5 billion more each year. Good grief!*

Uncle Dave would like to caution you to keep your original goals modest. If you try to save too much money too fast, it may prove impossible to maintain the pattern. Then you will be tempted to take some of the money back out when you need it, thereby subverting your objective. Finally, remember this: In the beginning, the amount you save is not as important as the habit you develop. Perhaps this true story will make the point effectively.

> *Mathew is one of my real-life nephews. I began discussing finances with him when he was a high school student, washing dishes part-time at a nearby restaurant. Since he was too young to have bad financial habits, he was immediately successful. At first, he could only save $5 per week, but he did it religiously. Before long he got a better job and saved even more. Each time he got a raise or a new job he would save about half of his additional income and use the other half to raise his standard of living. By the time he graduated from college (he paid for that too), he had enough money to buy his first home. Before long he rented that home out and bought another one. Then he bought another rental property.*

> *By his late 20's he accumulated a net worth of more than $75,000. Then he got married. Heather quickly jumped on board with the program. Six years later, they have two lovely children and doubled their nest egg. Mathew is 33, Heather just celebrated her 30th birthday: very impressive.*
>
> *All of this started on a dishwasher's salary. Now they are entering their prime earning years. They have excellent financial habits and ought to be able to redouble their net worth every 6-8 years.*

How Much Is $100 per Month Really Worth?

Earlier, I asked that question. The answer is "somewhere around $17,000, depending on interest rates." We touched on this idea earlier. Let's suppose you can put $100 per month into an investment that pays 7%. After 10 years, you will have accumulated $17,000. By reinvesting that $17,000 at the same 7%, you will enjoy $1,200 per year in new interest income, which equals $100 per month. So, $100 per month for 10 years at 7% equals $17,000 and $17,000 at 7% equals $100 per month.

You can manipulate these numbers for your amusement, but the exact numbers here are not especially germane. What you need to understand is $100 per month is a lot more than it seems like. For every $100 per month in reliable income you can generate and/or save consistently, you have gotten somebody else to pay a significant part of your debt for you—debt which you hate… remember? There are lots of people who can do that for you. You will meet them in the next chapter.

I hope you can now understand just how powerful $100 per month can be. That is why other companies are always trying to collect their income from you. NO MORE! It is time to turn the coin over and put the eighth wonder of the world (compound interest) to work FOR YOU by saving consistently.

Step 3 – INVEST WISELY

> *An investor can buy a typical townhome as a rental and watch it drop in value by half its original cost and still make a nice profit. How can that be? The answer will follow later.*

Naturally, Uncle Dave thinks real estate is the best way for all of us ordinary folks to build an empire. I call the best reasons "Power Points." Let's check out the top three Power Points and discover why you are going to begin investing in real estate. Knowing this information will also enable you to work with investors.

POWER POINT #1 - Four Distinct Profit Centers (and a Bonus)

There are so many different ways to make money with your real estate investments it takes several pages to explain them all. Consider these:

Cash Flow

Cash flow is any money that is left over after paying everything and everybody. Believe it or not, it is possible to have too much cash flow. The tax man loves investors with lots of cash flow. It is taxed as ordinary income and that can get fairly expensive. If you find yourself in this situation consider refinancing your property and buying another one with the proceeds or trade your property for something bigger. Either way, you get to invest your money, rather than give it away unnecessarily.

Principal Reduction

If you have ever seen an amortization schedule you know that in the early months of a loan most of the payment goes to interest, and a very small amount pays down the loan. As the months and years drip by, the amount that goes to principal climbs slowly but surely. When the borrower gets near the end of the schedule, the principal pays off quickly. Since Uncle Dave likes real estate as a long-term investment, I am very happy with that system.

> *Controlled debt is one key to your wealth.*

If very humble people manage to pay off their homes over time, it is easy to believe that somebody with modest ambition (you) could buy a few similar homes and rent them out over a couple of decades. Your tenants will give you money to save consistently, through principal reduction of your loans, and eventually they will help you to transform your debt from a liability into equity. That new equity is then available to you for any purpose you wish, hopefully for additional investments. Time is going to pass anyway, so why not take advantage of it?

All of this is an example of a very important financial concept called "controlled debt." For our purposes controlled debt is any debt that you can realistically expect somebody else to pay off for you. Therefore, if you would like to eventually become a millionaire, all you need to do is accumulate one million dollars in "controlled" debt and let somebody else pay it off for you, over time.

In the end, Uncle Dave considers the built-in forced-savings program of principal reduction to be a severely under-appreciated profit center.

Tax Savings

People who own investment properties generally pay lower income taxes than other people who earn the same amount of income but do not have investment properties. For starters, the investor gets to deduct all real expenses necessary to run the property. This includes things like taxes, interest, utilities, paint, management fees and travel expenses to show the property to prospective tenants.

The bigger benefit comes in the form of depreciation. In essence, the investor gets to claim that the property is slowly falling apart even if it is not. On a $100,000 property the investor could easily enjoy $1,000 per year in real tax savings just from this write-off.

Another issue has to do with capital gains tax. Some investors like to refinance their properties whenever the cash flow gets too great because they can use that money, free of taxes, for a long time or forever. If they decide to sell the property later, the taxes they owe will most likely be considered capital gains tax, which can be half as much as ordinary income tax. Therefore, it is better to make profits off of investments than commissions from hard work.

Finally, Uncle Dave should advise the reader that this tax stuff can be a little tricky. For example, there is a problem when you sell a property that you have been writing off; it is called recapture tax. Another issue lies in the fact that tax benefits vary based on the investor's income bracket. Until such time as you have a very good handle on the various twists, be sure to consult a tax expert each time you are involved in a real estate investment.

Appreciation

A dog may be a man's best friend, but when it comes to the investor's best friend, our warm-hearted tail-wagging buddies take a back seat to appreciation. This delightful profit center takes two forms: natural and forced. The natural source for increased property values comes from standard inflation. The government institutes policies to encourage inflation and, therefore, appreciation of property.

For example, the U.S. government is the biggest debtor and it likes a modest inflation rate because it can pay back its debt with cheaper dollars. In addition, it likes to see citizens get modest pay raises because that new-found income moves the citizens into higher tax brackets and generates more revenues. The primary way the Feds manipulate inflation (and appreciation of property) is through interest rates. (If you would like to know more about how the government deals with inflation, look up "M2 money supply.")

JOKE TIME - Two brokers were taking their ethics exam. When the instructor left the room, one broker leaned over to the other broker and whispered, "Psst, what did you get for number two?"

Local governments also like to see property values increase. Higher real estate prices mean higher property tax revenues for them to spend.

City, county, state and federal governments all benefit when property values rise because citizens will refinance their homes to pull that equity out. When they do that, they buy new and bigger homes or other things and as a result they stimulate the economy.

If an investor buys a $100,000 townhome and it drops in value by half of its original cost he or she can still make a profit.

In most cases the investor/buyer puts in a down payment of something like 20% of the original purchase price. If the property has dropped in value to $50,000 when his or her tenants finally pay off his or her loan, he or she has still made $30,000 in profit. Furthermore, the investor may have pocketed cash flow and tax benefits along the way. No other investments can do that because they do not allow for the same leverage that real estate does.

The real estate market is directly affected by these policies. New home prices climb when the costs of building materials and labor grow higher. As those homes rise in value, the pre-owned homes are cheaper by comparison, so certain people are drawn to them instead. All of that extra demand for the pre-owned homes forces their value up as well.

Over time, natural appreciation can be very significant but "forced appreciation" can be even more substantial.

The best way to create value is to buy below market in the first place. You can also buy properties that need to be fixed up. You can put on an addition, or finish off a basement or attic. Sometimes you can add value by changing zoning or converting apartments into condominiums or subdividing land. Occasionally, you can combine more than one type of forced appreciation. Uncle Dave has done all of these, some of them many times.

Broker Bonus

There is a fifth profit center, which is available only to licensees: commissions. Agents who invest on their own account can pick up a couple percent of the sales price when buying their properties and a similar amount when selling them. In some cases, the net commission can exceed one or more of the other profit centers offered by a particular investment. Sometimes, this bonus profit center can make a borderline deal more appealing. Additionally, the broker might be able to structure the transaction so that his or her money is a capital gain rather than earned-income, and reduce the overall tax burden. Not bad.

When we review the 4 Profit Centers that are available to investors of real estate, it is obvious why so many average folks pick this investment over all others.

POWER POINT # 2 – Compounding Your Effectiveness

Another financial benefit to real estate vs. other investments lies in your ability to utilize OPM (other people's money) and OPT (other people's time). OPM and OPT work for both investors and brokers.

> **OPIUM is the acronym for O.P.M., which stands for Other People's Money. You can acquire lots of OPIUM by finding and sharing the best deals.**

One of the most common ways to use OPM is when a borrower uses a lender's money to create "leverage." The fact that one can finance such a large part of real estate investments serves to compound the investor's rate of return. For example, if I were to buy a $100,000 duplex for all cash and rent out the units for $500 each per month, I would receive $12,000 per year or 12% on my money. But if you were to put $25,000 down on the same property you would have a loan of $75,000 and pay something like $5,200 per year for interest, thereby leaving you with $6,800 per year ($12,000 in income minus $5,200 interest) which is 27% on your investment. This is a fine example of leverage.

Another fantastic way to use OPM has to do with tenants. Over time, the tenant brings rent checks to the investor and eventually that pays the loan down (passive income) and thereby transforms a liability into equity, which can be converted to cash.

Partners also have money that can be used to compound an investor's effectiveness. When it comes to investing in real estate, you can make more money by sharing half the profits with partners than you can by investing as an individual and keeping all the money for yourself. Here is why.

Let's start out by assuming you can earn $75,000 per year in commissions and you need $55,000 to pay all of your living expenses and the IRS. Obviously, that leaves you with $20,000 to invest. That is a nice sum and it might buy you one nice property, but it is small potatoes compared to the money other people have. So, the goal here is to get those other people to use their money to buy lots of half-properties for you. Uncle Dave will show you how to do that in the next chapter.

OPM is also used by brokers in the traditional line of duty. Whenever you take a new listing, the seller becomes your partner and a source of OPM. You get the top 6% or so of the sales price, in exchange for your services. The buyer is also a source of OPM for brokers because they bring all the money to the table and brokers get some of it. God bless 'em!

Other People's Time (OPT) is the kissing cousin of OPM and the other primary way to compound your effectiveness. You are no different than a business owner who employs a secretary, a manager or a janitor to help run the company. Neither of you can do everything yourself so you will do better if you use OPT.

As your business grows you may decide that a personal assistant can help handle paper work. After that you may even need a licensed assistant to work with some of your extra buyers.

As you accumulate some rental properties you will quickly discover the value of property managers and maintenance people. And then there are our wonderful allies, the tenants. Whenever tenants go to work, they devote large blocks of their time to the cause and then bring their landlord the fruits of their labor. These are all examples of using OPT.

Since tenants are so prominent in both categories (OPM and OPT) they deserve a place of honor within this heading. Three cheers for tenants! YIPPEE! YAHOO! HOORAY!

POWERPOINT # 3 – Cooperation and Competition

Cooperation and competition may seem contrary to one another but they are each an integral part to the typical real estate transaction. Prior to the formation of NAR, in 1908, it was normal for a listing broker to represent both buyer and seller in any specific transaction. But many buyers were not comfortable with that arrangement because they wanted to have their own agents represent them. Therefore NAR observed that the public is served best when Realtors share their listings with each other. This pooling of sellers and buyers is what NAR means when they use the term "cooperate." That is also where the term "co-op fee" comes from.

Once that listing is secured, "competition" for that one-of-a-kind property serves the seller plus fast-acting brokers and buyers. The listing broker only has 3 days to post a listing with the Multiple Listing Service, but in the meantime a lot can happen. If the broker knows a prospective buyer for the listing he or she can try to put a fast transaction together; or, if he or she mentions the listing at a sales meeting other brokers can move quickly if they know someone else who might complete that transaction. But the fuse is short.

> *Insider trading is illegal in the stock market, but real estate brokers are free to utilize inside information for their investors or for their own accounts.*

The overwhelming majority of listings are entered into the Multiple Listing Service. Once that happens it is presumed that all agents have equal access to the information, even though most of them have no real knowledge of the matter. Agents who are paying close attention have an inside track to the hot deals for their buyers. Other buyers are locked out because their own brokers have not seen the listing yet, or the buyers haven't lined up financing or they cannot look at the property until the weekend or until their own home sells, etc. Brokers aren't the only ones competing.

- The buyer competes with the seller to see who can get the best deal.
- The sellers have to compete with other sellers for buyers.
- Buyers have to compete with each other for the inventory.

If you have ever heard of a "buyers' market," you have seen competition at work from that angle. Whenever the sellers are forced to compete for the few buyers, investors can make multiple offers and only accept very good deals. Oh, happy days!

The inside track to good deals is an incredibly powerful benefit for real estate buyers and investors. That is all set up by a combination of cooperation and competition.

Real Estate vs. the Stock Market

Whenever Certified Financial Planners discuss investing, they rarely focus on anything other than stocks and bonds. Uncle Dave contends their one-sided philosophy is either ignorant or dishonest. These "experts" tell us things like diversify, stay in it for the long run, and use options to control risk. But diversification diminishes your successes and exposes you to more opportunities to lose. The long run is a philosophy used to recover losses, but clinging to past problems in hopes they improve is like watering weeds and hoping they produce fruit. Options are complicated and lend additional ways to lose your money.

Anybody who has been in the stock market long enough knows it is more like gambling than investing, and bonds represent saving, not investing. Here are some other points:

There are limited tax benefits to buying stocks.
You cannot get tenants to buy stocks for you
You cannot get partners to buy stocks for you.
Leverage opportunities are limited.
You cannot force the value of stocks to go up.

On the other hand, more people are millionaires as a result of real estate than any other asset. Why fight it?

Wrapping up, this chapter is all about growing your middle, which is an enormous reward for getting your finances under control. We have observed that to do that an agent needs to HATE DEBT, SAVE CONSISTENTLY, and INVEST WISELY. Under the category of Invest Wisely, we established that real estate is the best investment because it has Three Power Points: 1) Profit

Centers 2) Compounding Effectiveness 3) and Cooperation and Competition. This group is so overwhelming that there is practically no justification for investing in anything else, especially for real estate professionals because they enjoy the inside track to so many good deals.

So now you are at an important crossroads. You can enter the business and struggle like so many others or you can use Uncle Dave's financial system as means to financial security and wealth. I am not asking you to work harder or to complete more deals. I am simply asking you to put yourself first and use the money you do make in a wiser way than you might otherwise do. If you do that, you will reap enormous rewards. In the next chapter I will show you how to do all this much faster than you ever imagined. You've gotta love that third leg of the Stool of Knowledge.

Now here is an interesting true story that was made possible because of the things we just discussed.

Uncle Dave's True Story #9: A Million from Trash

In 1997 Uncle Dave was looking around to buy a mid-sized apartment building when I got a call from Stan, who was a commercial broker. He had two brand-new listings in a very nice older area of Denver. Each property had 12 units.

Stan told me that the elderly woman who owned the properties lived out of state. The buildings had been in her family for years and usually provided her with some monthly income, but they were not doing that any longer. Her advisors inspected the buildings and discovered so many problems they knew she did not have the time, ability or resources to bring them back to their former glory. Understandably, they insisted she unload the properties as soon as possible.

The first property was on Columbine Street. Five of the units were vacant and there were rumors that the manager was a doper. Otherwise, the property was in decent-but-not-great shape. The asking price was $240,000. I knew that if I changed the manager, spruced up the street appeal and replaced the hall carpets, I could get the vacant units rented and create some cash flow as well as a handsome paper profit.

The other building was more interesting. It was on Marion Street, just one block from a popular park. The entire building was vacant and the ground-level windows were boarded up. The property had a larger parking lot than is normal in the area and there were several abandoned vehicles taking advantage of the scarce off-street parking.

An inspection of the interior of the building revealed a very odd problem. The laundry room was jam-packed with dozens of old bicycles and bicycle parts. But that was just the precursor of what was to follow. As we progressed through the inspection, nine of the vacant units presented the exact same picture. Dozens and dozens of bicycles were stuffed in all those apartments. I would guess there were two hundred of them all together. In addition, there were hundreds of extra tires, old seats, handlebars and other parts packed into the corners and closets.

We later learned that the former managers were "dumpster divers." Other big cities have the same type of people. They roam up and down the alleys, looking through the trash dumpsters for useful items. It must have taken them years to accumulate that massive inventory. We determined that at some point the managers started piling their booty in one of the units, which then became unrentable. When they ran out of "storage space" they simply confiscated a different apartment. Eventually, there was nothing left to rent out and all the income was lost.

The mass of bicycles made it difficult to see the units very well, so I was uncertain what type of repairs were needed. I knew it would cost a lot of money and take an enormous effort to get the property operating again. But the building was in a premium area so I reasoned if the price was reasonable, it might be an interesting project. Stan understood the situation perfectly. He listed the property for $120,000 so that there would be a sufficient incentive for somebody to take on the task.

After we finished our inspection, Stan asked what I thought about the two listings. I knew that this was a worthwhile endeavor for me, so I immediately responded, "I am going to pay you the respect of recognizing you have listed these properties correctly in the first place. Therefore, I will pay full price for both of them, and close quickly, so that the elderly woman can get the money she desperately needs. Furthermore, to show you I appreciate your bringing this opportunity to me first, I am not going to share in the commissions, even though I am a broker myself."

We wrote up the contract right there on his hood and it was accepted later that afternoon. When we were at the closing a few weeks later, Stan mentioned that a couple of other agents from his office were mildly upset with him because he told me about the properties before they learned of them, but I thought he did the smart thing. He knew that I had the resources to complete a quick deal and the experience to solve the problems. By calling me first, his client received full price and a quick sale, so he served her very well. In addition, he was able to keep the full commission for himself. His actions seemed wholly appropriate to me.

Back to the buildings: At the Columbine property, we immediately replaced the manager and some unseemly tenants. Then we put some spit and polish in the corners. Within a few months the property was fully occupied and operating effectively. Five years later, I traded that property for a bigger building and enjoyed a very nice profit of $200,000.

The Marion building required much more effort. Whenever we take over a run-down apartment building we have a very clear procedure. First, we fix any safety issues; then we work on the street appeal. After that, we attend to the common areas; finally we work on the vacant units.

In order to fix the broken windows and discover any safety concerns we had to get rid of all those two-wheelers.

We ordered a large construction dumpster and called a salvage dealer. We quickly filled the dumpster with bikes and the salvage guy hauled them off to sell for scrap metal. Within a week the bicycles were gone, the windows were fixed and the other urgent repairs were attended to. The property was safe, completing our first priority.

It only took two days to put in new sod, plus a small flower garden and matching evergreen trees on either side of the front sidewalk. After that, we painted the hallways and installed new carpeting. With that completed, we attacked the four apartments which were on the middle level of the three-story building. As soon as they were completed, we advertised for a resident manager. By the time the dust settled, it took about four months to get from the closing date to a fully operational apartment building.

Seven years later the area was in high demand and this building was ideal for conversion to condominium units. We attended to the legal matters, then vacated the property and gutted the building. We upgraded the laundry room and the hallways, reflecting a top-notch property. Then we upgraded all the condominium units to a first-class level. We provided new kitchens with new cabinets, granite countertops and stainless steel appliances. The bathrooms got new tile and luxury bathtubs. The remainder of the space was highlighted with features like hardwood floors, new windows, new carpets, new fixtures and cove molding. Then we designated one unit as a model and decorated it with new furniture. Those charming little condos sold as fast as we finished them.

The total sales price for all twelve units was slightly over $1,600,000. After deducting for remodeling costs, marketing and the original purchase price, that building served up a profit of slightly over one million dollars. And of course, there was the $200,000 that was made off the Columbine building. All things considered, "a million from trash" was a worthwhile endeavor, indeed.

Think about it. What did you learn?

Hint: Consider Uncle Dave's three-step system for financial success, the negotiation process and relationships with brokers.

Go to page 220 for your Instant Experience.

Chapter 10 – CRUMMY DOGS, FAT CATS & YOUR BEST CLIENT
or
Your Yellow Brick Road to Retirement

Most people would agree that the financial principles of the previous chapter (Hate Debt, Save Consistently and Invest Wisely) make a lot of sense, but true financial security might seem unattainable to you because it seems like it takes so long. Well, take a seat and buckle your seat belt. You are about to take a ride on the fast track.

> *You should read through and understand this chapter, even if you are unable or unwilling to employ the ideas yourself. You will meet investors along the way and some of them don't even know this stuff. If you can talk intelligently about these concepts you will earn their business and be rewarded for your knowledge.*

Whenever I am invited to speak at real estate offices, I always ask the agents, "Who is your best client?" Most of them pick a repeat client or somebody who is easy to work with, or a high-ticket buyer. I cannot recall any brokers who said they are their own best client.

129

One of the greatest benefits to securing a license lies in your inside track to inventory. While everybody from accountants to zoo keepers are busy at work, you can be shopping for opportunities that offer multiple thousands of dollars in profits. This extraordinary opportunity is simply too precious to waste. Later in the chapter, Uncle Dave will explain how and why one of the best ways to invest is to team up with other investors, but in the interim I would like to illustrate just how vital this is.

There were some very dynamic brokers working at the RE/MAX office from which I retired. At least half of them earned $100,000 per year (some of them made a lot more) in a market with a median home price of $200,000. I usually completed between 25 and 30 transactions each year but my average sales price was quite a bit below theirs. When the rankings came out at the end of the year, it always appeared I was among the lower ones within that group, but, as the saying goes, "The devil is in the details."

In approximately 1/4 of my transactions I was a principal (either the buyer or the seller) as well as a broker. Uncle Dave had a reputation of being a creative fellow, so there were plenty of occasions when my broker friends introduced me to their oddball or low-priced listings in hopes of making a quick deal. It was a type of farming technique for me. The reduced commission checks from transactions like that may have brought down the average commission checks for me, but the profit dollars were incredible.

In a sense, all brokers were working for me, even if they didn't know me. Their assignment was to go out and find me some good deals and post them in the Multiple Listing Service (MLS). All I had to do was keep an eye out for the opportunities they dug up.

Well, anyway, I made a ton of money picking up the profits that other brokers and their clients handed out like Halloween candy. To this day I still own a handful of free and clear rental properties that I bought that way.

> *Obviously, I do not know exactly who is reading this, when you are reading it or where you reside. Therefore, "crummy dogs" may not be available in your particular market now or ever. But that is not the point. What you are looking for is an opportunity to create cash flow or generate net worth by playing the wholesale/retail game. There are nearly always some great opportunities lurking in any market. By being your own best client, you will be able to grab them before somebody else does.*

Naturally, I loved it whenever I found opportunities like that, but my preferred investment of that time played an even bigger role in reducing my average commission check.

Uncle Dave held a special fondness for crummy little one-bedroom condos (the "dogs"), which could be picked up for $30,000 or so. A condo like that would rent for $595, which is 2% of the purchase price (it is extremely difficult to get that fantastic ratio on higher-priced properties). After paying all of the monthly expenses, this little property spins off a modest sum of slightly over $100 per month in cash flow, and that is the "equivalent" of $17,000. In addition, I picked up some "controlled debt" that tenants would turn into "real money" over time. (It is all starting to make sense, isn't it?)

So, while my talented broker friends were earning around $5,000 each time they sold a median priced home, I was making the equivalent of $17,000 each time I bought a boring little one-bedroom "dog."

After doing that 5-8 times per year for six years, I had accumulated a large pack of dogs and a base income of approximately $40,000 per year which was the equivalent of $566,666. I also had twice that much in controlled debt, which was destined to become real money via principal reduction. Due to favorable tax laws (see the previous chapter) that $40,000 in annual income was sheltered from income taxes. Since I had a property manager to attend to the details, I got my income without any additional effort on my part, an excellent example of "passive income."

Once I reached that point, my talented buddies had to work hard for several months each year before they matched my automatic base income of $40,000/year. In fact, they needed to sell about 11 homes (the average Realtor sells 10 homes per year), and give the IRS a big chunk before they also earned $40,000. When the next January rolled around, they had to bark up that same old tree again, and every year thereafter. While they were busy completing all those transactions, my tenants were paying off my controlled debt and increasing my net worth. Uncle Dave will freely admit those special brokers got more attention at the awards banquets than I did, and I genuinely admired their accomplishments, but I certainly did not envy them.

Over time, I was able to combine the base income from my "dogs" with a nice salary which my wife earned, and by living sensibly we had more than enough money to raise our family. But, I did not stop there. I kept working and nearly every new dollar I earned, either as commissions or profits, was available for more investing. Can you imagine how powerful that is?

Meet Eric

One of the brokers with whom I worked at that time was Eric. He called me just this week. It was nice to hear from him again. Seven years have passed since the last time we spoke. In that time he moved to Texas and discovered he likes to sell small ranches. After many years of grinding out commissions, he finally realized he needed to rethink his priorities. After all those years and a string of bad luck he was essentially still at square one. With no savings, no new ideas and subpar credit, he asked me if I could help him. Naturally, I was honored that he sought my counsel.

We spent some high-quality time together and I explained my simple system to him as I have done to so many others before him—the same system I am going to share with you. This system will enable him to retire within fifteen years, even though he has no extra money and limited credit at this time. After a one-hour crash course, Eric immediately knew how he could modify the concept to work within his market. Later, he sent me the following email.

Grammar freaks take note: At the time this was written, neither Eric nor I had any idea his email would end up in here, so please forgive the imperfections.

Dave,

One of the more compelling thoughts that has come into my mind following our discussion today is the realization that I knew you 15 years ago when we were working side by side at RE/MAX Professionals in Denver.

If I would have followed a charter similar to the one we discussed today, putting my money in the "middle category" by paying myself first all those years, my financial troubles today would probably not exist. The hardest pill to swallow is knowing those years are gone by.

However, I am grateful for your advice and at the risk of sounding patronizing, I want you to know that I have a great deal of respect for you personally. This is because I know that you have "earned" the knowledge you so freely were willing to share.

I have heard that no man knows anything until they reach 50 (which I did this year). In some ordinary and unusual ways I am beginning to understand the true meaning of those words and the "student" in me seems to be finding new "teachers" more frequently.

With that being said, I have taken immediate

action on the plans we discussed today. I am starting my "target list" of potential partners and I am going to the bank for my 1st monthly "savings deposit" RIGHT NOW. . . I will keep you posted.

THANKS FOR THE INSPIRATION!

Eric

Eric's letter reveals a universal truth that all of us know but very few people sufficiently appreciate: Time is going to pass by without any regard for our personal choices. Therefore, we can either find ways to let it to work for us, or ignore it as it slowly steals away our youth and our best opportunities. I am very pleased Eric has discovered how to build a brighter future for himself.

I have shared this simple concept with many agents and most of them "get it" when we get this far. I hope you are getting a little bit excited, too. However, if you are like them, there is a good chance this all seems scary to you. After all, you were merely looking for ways to become a more effective broker, not some hotshot investor.

You are probably thinking that there is no way you can start investing without deeper pockets—much deeper pockets. But your trusty uncle has good news for you: I am going to tell you how to employ this concept, even if you have no money and bad credit.

So, let's enjoy some time together discussing exactly how you can become your own best client and accumulate passive income, regardless of your circumstances. Get out your highlighter. Here we go.

> *We both get something we could not get without the other person.*

How to Become Your Own Best Client

To begin with, Uncle Dave would like to ask you a question:

Do you agree that agents have the inside track to the best deals? If not, I urge you to review the True Stories at the end of each chapter. If you believe it, you are on the path to wealth by becoming your own best client. Here is how to begin.

Step One - Find the Fat Cats (A group of cats is called a "clowder.")

The first thing you need to do is identify a list of potential partners. These Fat Cats (your clowder) do not have to be filthy stinking rich. They just need to have good jobs, a small savings account and a desire to make some profits. Perhaps you have friends or family members who make a respectable living and could use some tax breaks. Ask your accountant if any of his clients would like to reduce their tax burden. If you have already been in the business a while, you probably know past clients who make a good living. Identify any other successful people with whom you have contact, such as the grocery store manager or the principal at your child's school. If you cannot come up with at least eight people to contact, you can send mail into upper middle class areas to find candidates.

Once you have identified 8-20 potential partners you are ready to begin a little "farm" and contact them. Your presentation and their likely response will go something like this:

> *"Linda, do you have all the money you need or could you use some extra dollars?"*
>
> *(giggles) "I could always use more money, Uncle Dave. Why do you ask?"*
>
> *"Well, I am in the real estate business and I have an inside track to some fantastic deals, and I am looking for a couple partners to share them with me."*
>
> *"Why do you need me?"*
>
> *"I cannot afford to buy all of them by myself, but sometimes the cash flow (or purchase price) is just too good to pass up, so I am willing to share them with*

certain people because I would rather have half a pie than no pie at all."

"That makes sense. How would it work?"

"Well, I am not trying to sell anything. I am just trying to identify some people who would like to team up to make some good money."

"My boss might be interested, but I need to know a little more."

"Sure. Whenever a good deal shows up, you or your boss would put up the down payment and obtain the loan. I will manage the property for 5 years. At the end of that time, we sell or refinance the property. You guys get your money back first and then I get paid for my property management. After that we split whatever is left over, 50/50."

"That sounds like a good idea, but why don't you just do it yourself?"

"I would like to, but there is a limit to how many loans I can get and what I can qualify for by myself. But by working together, we both get something we could not get without the other person. You get my best deals plus a devoted manager who has the time and skill to solve the day-to-day problems. I get a small commission and half-property for sharing my best deals and handling all the details."

"That seems fair. What happens if I change my mind and need my money back?"

"We have a simple, but legal, Partnership Agreement to address those items, but we're getting a little ahead of ourselves. I was just wondering if you would like to hear about my best deals."

"It sure wouldn't hurt to listen. Okay, if you find something good give me a call. I might consider it."

"Cool, perhaps we can make each other some extra money sometime. I will keep you posted."

If you approach it like that, nearly everybody will want to hear about the best opportunities. If this person has the ability to perform, or knows somebody who does, you have landed a good prospect. Now go get another one. Once you have about 8 Fat Cats in your clowder who are "willing to listen" you are ready for step two.

JOKE TIME - A real estate broker and a seedy character had had a few too many at the local bar when the Realtor started complaining that he was unable to locate a nice two-story home for one of his clients. Then the other fellow said "You're in luck. I have the perfect home for you. It is a two-story of 4,000 square feet. It sits on 10 acres. It has a fantastic view and I might accept $50,000 for it." Naturally, the Realtor got very excited and asked to see it right away. They piled into the broker's nice Mercedes and headed for the other man's home. When the Realtor arrived at the home, he quickly realized the other man's home was nothing more than a run-down shack. The indignant Realtor demanded an explanation and the other man responded, "My wife and I were driving around and she kept saying I am a no-good con-man; then, she threw me out of the car right by that bar."

"What the heck does that have to do with me?" demanded the Realtor.

"I told her I didn't need her to get back home; I would just get my chauffeur to bring me back. Thanks for the lift."

Step Two - Go Shopping

Now that you have some potential Fat Cats lined up, it is time to go on a treasure hunt. You are looking for something that offers good cash flow or that you can buy 15-20% below market. If you can talk with the listing agents before you go inspect properties to determine the sellers' motivation, you may be able to eliminate the sellers who are not going to be very flexible. If one of your Fat Cats wants to go with you to inspect the properties, that is fine, but you will probably move along quicker if you go by yourself. Do not rush this step. It is important to find something special.

Once you find a property that you can get excited about, move quickly because you want to seize on good deals before they get away.

Step Three - Let's Make a Deal

The negotiation process is very important. In normal transactions, an agent hauls a buyer around and once a suitable property is located, the buyer makes an offer and negotiations are under way. This time, things are a bit different.

> *Sometimes your best opportunities are found right within your own office.*

Uncle Dave likes to shop by himself and make offers in his own name, then allow for the right to assign the contract. So, the buyer is "Uncle Dave and/or Assigns." There are several reasons I approach the transaction this way. First, I can get the property off the market quicker than if I have to haul several potential buyers to the property and wade through all the usual rituals. Second, I don't want the partners to do the negotiations because they are scared and they will tend to make ridiculously low and unrealistic offers as a defense mechanism; and, most importantly, so that they yield control of the property and the entire process to me.

Your biggest challenge is to get past the biases of the listing agent. Some of them have not received an offer structured that way. They may want you to prove you can pay cash or obtain a loan. If you are incapable of doing that, all you need to do is tell them you have partners and you don't know which one you are going to work with. Therefore, you need 7 days or so to work out the details.

If the brokers suggest you just go get the buyer and show him or her to them, you will explain that there are several possible buyers and it is better and quicker to have the details worked out before they get involved. In addition, this way the seller gets a realistic price.

If the listor still resists you, it is probably because they don't want to take the property off the market without some certainty they have a real buyer. In that event, tell them you will allow them to continue marketing the property in search of some other buyer whom they like better until such time as you provide the information they seek. Make any reasonable concession to get the property under contract and in your name. If it just cannot be worked out this way, you can still approach the transaction the more traditional way and bring your prospects by one at a time. But you are giving up so much that Uncle Dave suggests you look for something else.

Before we move on, there are a few side points. First, if you can sincerely qualify for loans yourself or get one of your potential buyers to sign a contract in advance, the negotiation process is easier. Second, sometimes your best opportunities are found within your own office because your co-workers know you and might encourage their clients to be more accommodating. Third, if you ever deal directly with an owner who does not have a broker or legal representation it is essential to disclose in the contract that you are licensed and might make a profit. When the owner has a broker or attorney, that disclosure is not essential, but it is still a good practice.

It may take a few times at bat before you get a contract accepted, but somebody is motivated enough to do what you need, so don't give up. It is your job to find him or her. When you get to that point, be certain it is a very good deal. Then, it is time to gather your thoughts.

Step 4 - The Analysis

Take a moment to think about your potential partners and how they match up with this particular property. All partnerships do not have to be the same, and you do not need to split everything right down the middle. Remember: There are four profit centers (see previous chapter). They are all good for you. If one of your partners needs tax benefits more than you do, then let them have all of the tax benefits in exchange for your getting something else. Perhaps you could use your management fee as you go along rather than as a lump sum on the back end; or, you might take 60% of the eventual profits or all of the principal reduction. There are lots of possibilities so be flexible.

Once you have a handle on the range of possibilities, it is time to approach your Fat Cats, but think about who you should talk with first. Do you have any clues as to who is the most likely to join you? Do you prefer one over the other? Why? Uncle Dave suggests you speak with most of them before you approach your number one choice among them.

Naturally, you will be thrilled if one of them says they will take the deal before you get to your preferred Fat Cat, but most of them will want to "think about it" for a day or two. That is perfect. You are trying to do more than just force an early deal. You are trying to build a corral of partners and investors for the long run.

Once you have a clear grasp of the options, saddle up your pony; you are going for a ride.

Step 5 - The Presentation

There are several ways to handle this phase. One of my friends likes to invite several potential clients to his office at the same time, usually on a Saturday. Then he piles them all in the same minivan and drives them all to the same property. His approach is effective because many people are more comfortable with new ideas if they observe other people who like the idea too. As they feed off each other and gain enthusiasm, they create subtle competition among themselves. It should not surprise you he enjoys a very high success rate with his approach.

Uncle Dave likes more personal relationships and I am effective on the phone. I recognize that if they have never owned rental property before, they will be excited because of greed and apprehensive because of fear. I want to get the emotions out of it by keeping the concept simple and nonthreatening. I simply call them and remind them of our previous conversation. Then I tell them I found something they ought to look at, even if they are not ready, "just so they can see the type of deal we can do together." If I remain cavalier, they don't feel pressured. That is fine with me because I want them to trust me for the long term.

Remember, you are trying to accomplish more than simply selling this new investment. You are trying to plant seeds that grow into multiple transactions over the coming months and years. Some of your prospects need to see how the system works before they will act. This is your chance to educate them so they will be familiar and comfortable with you and the process the next time you call them. Invite them to bring somebody else if they wish. If a young woman brings her mother, the mom could be somebody whom you should meet. If a fellow brings his wife, she will undoubtedly need to know what is going on anyway, so this is a good chance to introduce her to the idea of investing. She may prove to be your greatest advocate.

Regardless of whether you take them to the property all at once as my friend does, or one at a time as I do, your objective is the same: to create the impression of demand. Don't hesitate to tell them others are looking at the deal. I take a nonchalant approach and say something like, "I am going to partner up with somebody on this one because it is too good to let it get away. You guys can join me if you want to, but don't sweat it if you're not ready, because it is the kind of deal Frank likes and I am meeting him later. I just wanted to show it to you first, in case you're interested." You will quickly know their level of interest. If they start probing you about the intricate details, chances are good that they are fairly interested, but if the conversation tends to remain more general, they are probably not ready.

If one of them wants the deal that is great, but if not, you have successfully planted the seeds for the next transaction and that is just as important. The more seeds you plant, the better.

Now it is time for your preferred Fat Cat. The procedure is essentially the same but the delivery is slightly different. It goes something like this: "I am going to partner up with somebody on this one because it is too good to let it get away. Bill and Nancy are interested but they are new to investing. I was sort of hoping you would be ready because you understand this stuff better, and that will be easier for me. Besides, I would rather share my best deals with somebody who can appreciate all the profit that is on the table."

If you read this person correctly, he should recognize you have produced a deal better than he would ever have found on his own. In addition, he has a devoted partner to handle the details, which he does not want to do. It is probably the best investment he has ever seen. If he wishes to buy the property without you, that is probably okay too. All that is left to do is decide who gets what, and you are already prepared for that conversation.

After that is resolved, you need to execute two documents. First, you should execute a Partnership Agreement (see Appendix One) which spells out the relationship. This will reduce the risk of misunderstandings later. Second, you need to Assign (see Appendix Two) the contract to your new partner. From there, you will provide his/her information to the listing broker and amend the original contract to establish who the final buyer is.

Step 6 – The Follow-Up

After the deal is locked up, quickly get back to your other prospective partners who saw the property and let them know how well it went. They should feel a hint of jealousy. Tell them you will be watching for the next great deal and you will call them when it arrives. Keep them posted as the transaction progresses. As soon as the place is rented out for cash flow or resold for a profit, call them again. As each phase is demystified, your credibility grows. Before long they will want to become the next preferred Fat Cat in your clowder.

Finally, you need to be constantly on the lookout for new and better partners. Whenever you meet somebody who seems modestly affluent and who could qualify for a loan, ask them the same thing you asked Linda earlier, "Do you have all the money you need or could you use some extra dollars?" Then tell them what just happened to your last investor, and offer to call them to see the next one.

Trailing Points

All of this may seem a bit complicated, but I assure you if you just take it one step at a time it unfolds naturally. It may take a while to put your first deal together, but once word gets out that your investor/partners are making money which they never made before, you will have plenty of repeat business and more Fat Cats in your clowder than good deals. That is when you will start putting bigger groups together to buy apartment buildings or other larger projects.

Next, the Partnership Agreement I have shared with you may not be the best one for you. I like it because it is succinct and nonthreatening, but you should have a conversation with an attorney (who specializes in real estate) to come up with your own document that works best for you. After you get that document, it is fairly easy to modify it as you begin working with different Fat Cats. Your attorney will be able to explain some of the tricky title issues when you get into transactions like this and the most effective ways to deal with them.

Next, the modest commission checks you make on these "crummy dogs" are moderately useful in the short-term, but do not abandon your other business. This is a long-term strategy that is designed to provide stable income and a retirement plan. It should be employed as a means to fill voids in your income whenever the market slows down and whenever you don't have some other hot prospect to serve. The rest of the time, Uncle Dave suggests you devote 80% of your time to matters which meet your immediate income needs and 20% of your time on this program. By adding 5-8 properties to your portfolio in each of 5-8 consecutive years, you should create a fabulous base income that will serve as your own yellow brick road to financial security and a most pleasant retirement.

Finally, you cannot get to the end without a beginning. If you are going to be your own best client, act like it. Begin by beginning! I suggest you review the previous chapter, then sit down right now and analyze your debt and bills to find a place you can stop wasting money. Commit to changing that one small thing. Then go immediately to the bank and put $100 in that new savings account we talked about. Put the deposit slip someplace obvious as a symbol of your new commitment. Then focus on developing smart habits rather than succumbing to the whims of life.

Then, get those Fat Cats and crummy dogs lined up and sincerely consider yourself to be your own best client.

Have you ever heard the old line, "The first million is the hardest one to make"? Well, I assure you it is true. The second one takes half as long to accumulate and each one thereafter takes even less time. Remember the message I shared with you very early in this book: If this lower-middle class, C student, double drop-out, bankrupt, prisoner with six sisters and a red real estate license can do it, you can too. I sincerely hope you will do it.

If you want to see how this concept works in real life, you will enjoy the following story.

Uncle Dave's True Story #10: The Parlay of 49th Avenue

In the middle and late 1980s, Colorado was one of several states that went through economic struggles due to shenanigans in the oil industry (sound familiar?) Real estate prices dropped dramatically. As expected, lower prices led to an abundance of foreclosures, which presented extra opportunities for three groups: first-time buyers, investors and brokers who specialized in selling that type of inventory.

Larry was one of the brokers in our office who observed that there were all kinds of new listings to be had. He joined forces with a national group that was retained to liquidate the glut of inventory. Even though prices were low and fewer normal folks were moving around, agents like Larry were able to maintain their income by filling in with the volume of cheap properties.

I was part of a less organized group: investors. I especially liked cheap condominiums because they provided cash flow and low risk, a delicious combination. I bought a bunch of them including about 15 or so with my friend, Bob. Over a three-year period, Bob and I bought several of Larry's listings.

Each time we went to the closing Larry complimented us for the wisdom of our concept. After several such experiences with Larry and other brokers, Bob wondered out loud, "If those guys know what a great idea it is, why don't they do it too?" We speculated that those brokers simply didn't want to be distracted by the management responsibilities.

One day around 1990, Larry got a new listing from his foreclosure network. It was a very modest one-bedroom condo in a decent part of town. He helped the seller by coordinating the repairs that the property required. After they finished the remodeling process, the little property had new floor coverings, paint, appliances, counter tops, window coverings and fixtures.

Obviously, it was very nice. Once the work was completed Larry told me about his listing. The asking price was a paltry $15,000.

Bob and I inspected the cute little condo and decided to make an offer. For some unknown reason Bob was feeling ornery, which was out of character for him. He suggested we offer the lender/seller $10,000 for the property. After I reminded him that the seller spent almost that amount fixing up the property, I suggested that such a low offer would probably make them angry. Bob's response was an all-time classic when he said, "Well, if they do get angry, they will have a long time to get over it." I liked his logic.

A few days later Larry told me that the bank had issued its counter offer of $13,000. I was dumbfounded. That was an absolute steal for that little property. I quickly called Bob with the good news and for some reason, which still eludes me, Bob suggested we look for something else. I went with the flow. Thirty days later, Larry told me the bank reconsidered. He inquired, "Would you guys be willing to pay $10,900?" I almost felt guilty! Almost! We accepted the counter offer. Bob and I agreed to be partners once again. I was the manager and he put up the down payment.

At that price, we could have paid cash for the condo, but we decided to put $4,000 down and get a loan of $7,000 from a local bank. The loan officer was Clark. Two weeks passed and we still had not heard from Clark about our loan approval so I called him to get an update. When I inquired about the loan status, he informed me they elected not to make the loan. Naturally, I asked him, "Why not?" Clark's response was nearly as priceless as that earlier remark of Bob's. Clark responded, "Anything that cheap can't be any good."

I suggested he get off his butt and go inspect the property. That did the trick. One week later we went to Clark's office to complete the paperwork and receive a check for the desired sum. When the signing ceremony was complete, Clark followed me to my car and probed, "Can you get me any of those?" I politely told him, "No, if we found any similar properties we would be able to buy them ourselves."

From there, I took the check and met Bob and Larry at the closing. We turned over the $7,000 we got from Clark and $4,000 which Bob provided. After the usual procedures, I pocketed a very small commission check and Larry repeated his earlier sentiments, "Boy, you guys are really doing the right thing." We agreed!

The property was so nice it rented up right away. We paid off Clark's loan within a few years and enjoyed cash flow from the free and clear property for several years after that. In addition, the market was starting to improve. Eventually, I bought out Bob and continued to enjoy cash flow and appreciation for another five years or so. Then I traded that modest condominium for a mid-sized apartment building.

Think about it. What did you learn?

Hint: Consider the roles of Larry, Bob and Clark.

Go to page 221 for your Instant Experience.

Chapter 11 – ON YOUR MARK, GET SET . . .
or
Office before License

If you already have a license and you are satisfied with where you work, you may be tempted to skip over this section, but don't go away before you read the True Story at the end of the chapter. It is a good one.

For the rest of you, this chapter will help you to gain a big head start on your first day. Let's examine why you should pick out your office before you obtain a license, as well as the best ways to acquire each of them.

As your career progresses, you will develop clients who know you, trust you and like you. Eventually, they will think of you first and the company for which you work will become secondary to them. Once you have enough relationships like that, you can move to nearly any office you wish, and your client base will follow you. But until that time, your original affiliation is critical.

> *It is a good idea to live together for a while before you get married.*

The relationship between the agent and the first office is like a marriage, so you don't want to rush into it. However, few agents lend sufficient thought to this topic until they have their license in hand, and that is too cavalier. Uncle Dave hopes readers of this book will take a smarter approach and investigate all their options before they get their licenses. It is a good idea to live together for a while before you get married.

There is a lot to learn about a firm before you can be certain you are well matched. You need to examine their market share, their business style, their reputation, their training programs, whether they provide leads for you and a lot more. You need to learn where the bathroom is and where the forms are kept. You need to learn all the office policies and meet your support staff and fellow agents. Then there are office procedures, computer programs and telephone systems. There are business cards and yard signs to order. You should visit the home office if there is one.

You are not done yet. You still need to align yourself with a title company and a lender or two. Don't forget all that preliminary research like gaining familiarity with the lender's loan products. And of course you will need to identify a client list and a marketing plan. After all that is completed, most brokers are still several months away from their first payday.

Imagine a gardener who goes to a nursery: She picks out a great tomato plant, brings it home, prepares the soil, and plants it. Then she decides that watering the plant is a bit inconvenient so instead of watering, she decides to sit down and "hope" the plant knows it should bear fruit for her.

As silly as that sounds, it is exactly what many new licensees do. They go to school, obtain a license, join an office, go to work and set up a client list. Then instead of making enough contacts to make their garden grow, they take a seat and "hope" somebody will call them with some business.

In spite of all those challenges, let's assume you are fortunate enough to find a qualified buyer within four weeks. It can easily take several more weeks to locate a suitable home for them and a similar period of time to get their loan in place and to complete their due diligence process (i.e., they have a fair chance to investigate the title, neighborhood issues, crime statistics, churches, schools, etc.). And none of that allows for time the sellers may need to locate their replacement property.

If your first client is a seller, the whole procedure takes even longer. There is no "standard" listing period, but it is not uncommon for listings to be for six months or so. There is a reason or that. It can easily take that long to locate an acceptable buyer. Some of the reasons include market conditions, seasonal concerns, over-priced listings, the seller doesn't keep the home looking nice, crashed transactions, family conflicts and more. Once a suitable offer is secured, it can easily take six weeks to complete the transaction and locate a replacement property. Whew!

Occasionally, there are interesting buy/sell chains: A wants B's home, but B won't sell until a suitable replacement home is located. Then B wants C's property, but C won't sell until a suitable replacement home is located. Then C wants D's property and so on. Each transaction is contingent on the other. If any part of the chain breaks, all of the transactions fizzle. Each buyer has a different lender, each seller has a different title company or escrow arrangement and each party has a different broker. The closings can be spread out over several places and a couple days. Throw in an attorney or two and a couple clerical errors and you have the makings of a very interesting experience.

That first transaction is wonderful, and you will probably remember it all the rest of your life, but unfortunately it is not enough. You have to have a chain of business before you can say you have made it. If you are like most people, it can easily take a full year to complete your personal apprenticeship and to get a reliable stream of flowing income.

Given all the obstacles of the first year, you cannot afford to spend any extra front-end months shopping for your first office or bouncing around in an office which is not well suited to you; and you certainly don't want to be pressured by time restraints and make a hasty choice which you might regret later. Given all those challenges, it just makes sense to locate your office and lay as much groundwork as possible, before you get your license. So, what should you do first?

Picking the Best Office for You

Most new agents expect to work in a traditional real estate office, selling pre-owned homes. There are countless opportunities in that regard but there is also plenty of competition for that business. Before the reader takes that common path it is recommended that the other options, identified in Chapter 13 of this book, be reviewed and considered. Several of the alternatives offer salaries and benefits that provide an effective way to phase into the business. If you have limited staying power or a low tolerance for risk, you might find those options appealing.

The next thing to consider is: Do you want to specialize in a particular part of town? If that is the case, there may be one company that is better suited to that market than all the others. If you have no such preference, you will give priority consideration to offices in your immediate neighborhood. There are probably some small companies in your area that would love to have you, but if they don't have someone who will hold your hand for several months and provide great personal training, it will be difficult to succeed there.

A larger local company, perhaps with several offices, might be a good candidate for you. The local company can be very dynamic if they have a hand-selected group of top–notch agents who will work closely with you. However, if they cannot give you the personal attention you need, you can probably find a better fit.

Some areas have Cooperative Offices. In this case a group of successful agents each forms their own personal company, usually one-man shops. They share common overhead, like rent, receptionist and janitorial expenses. Each broker makes his or her own office policies and can exploit his or her individuality while enjoying a well-known company name and an environment of successful brokers.

Some of those agents have spill-over business and will take on a beginner like you. Their name recognition and general success rate makes for a positive environment, but there is not much structure or organized training. If you are a self-starter, you can overcome that shortcoming by learning directly from them plus taking outside classes and reading on your own.

Some of those agents have spill-over business.

In the beginning, you will probably be a bit awkward so there is great comfort and value in aligning yourself with a name that the public knows and respects. That is why so many new agents find the franchises to be the most appealing place for their first position. In addition, these companies have effective systems in place plus occasional leads and regular training, all of which you need. The downside to these companies is there tends to be a fair number of sub-par performers hanging around who can distract you and stunt your progress if you let them.

Regardless of what you think your final choice is likely to be, it is a good idea to interview several brokers. This is the time to do that. There may be a hidden benefit in working for somebody that you did not consider. In addition to talking with the managing brokers, try to ask a couple of agents why they work there and if they think it is a good place for beginners. Ask about the manager's style and any extra benefits or challenges they know about.

> *SIZE MATTERS: What size office do you intend to work for? The smaller company means you can get more of the sales manager's time. They can be more flexible and you can get a larger percentage of "up-time" (whoever gets incoming calls). The larger companies offer name recognition, structured training, advertising budgets and other agents you can use for training on an "as-needed" basis. Unless you have some compelling reason to join a small company, Uncle Dave suggests you go where the training is best. But don't expect them to hand you any hot leads.*

So far we have discussed why it is important to shop for an office before you get your license and what type of offices there are from which to choose. Now it is time to explore the interview process. Be prepared with a resume and a list of questions. Asking questions is a key to success in the real estate business and this is your opportunity to make a good impression by showing you are not afraid to take control.

> *JOKE TIME - One lazy young broker was looking for a PDA or cell phone that would make his work easier so he went to the mall to find a suitable candidate. A clerk showed the broker a good model and said, "This baby will cut your work in half." So the lazy broker bought two of them.*

You will also be asked a group of predictable questions and perhaps an odd one or two. Generally, the questions are harmless and used to determine if you are confident and if you can think on your feet. Usually they will ask you why you want to get into the business and why they should hire you. They might want to know how much money you need to make, what you expect to do and what groups of people you know.

Answer their questions honestly, and try to use those questions as a tool for self-promotion. For example, if you are asked if you have children you can say something like, "Yes, I have two daughters. I really want to make enough money to give them some of the extras that life offers." Or, if they ask you what kind of work you have done in the past, you might say something like, "I worked in an office for an oil company, and it was boring because every day was the same. That is one reason I want to get into real estate, where no two days are alike."

One sales manager actually handed prospective agents a paperclip and asked the agents to sell it to him. He was looking for attitude, creativity and how they deal with the awkward moments. So, be prepared for unpredictable questions and approach the odd moments with good sportsmanship. If you can do that your manager knows she can teach you the technical stuff.

When it is your turn to ask questions, here are the key ones and some background information for you to pursue.

What are the company philosophies? Ask them about competition vs. cooperation. Can you compete with agents in your office for listings? How does the company interact with its competitors? Will they let you work with investors? What do they do if you buy or sell a home yourself? Do they protect areas where other agents specialize? What if you get a lead across the state or across the country?

If I represent a buyer or seller in a successful transaction, how is the commission split up? There is a wide range of possibilities. Some companies give you all of the commission but you have to pay monthly desk fees (perhaps $1,000 per month) plus all of your own expenses. Other companies charge you a transaction fee (something like $300 for each closing) plus 25% of each commission dollar. Still others simply split the fee, often on a 50-50 basis, but in that situation the company will usually pay for a lot of your expenses. There are all sorts of variations. Many companies have a full menu of split programs and you can even move from one to the other as your needs change.

Is there a set fee which I must charge my clients? Sometimes there is a lot of competition so flexibility can easily determine whether you get the listing or somebody else does. On the other hand, new agents tend to use price-cutting as a crutch and brokers are apprehensive about granting such flexibility.

Are there sales quotas? If you are paying monthly desk fees plus all your own expenses, you have a form of self-imposed pressure, so no quota is necessary. If you are on some sort of split program where the broker is paying your expenses, he will want to recapture his costs so some form of production may be required.

Who pays expenses? There are countless variations. Everything is open to negotiation, but you will usually have to pay your own Realtor dues, licensing fees, Errors and Omissions Insurance premiums and personal expenses like gas for your car and lunch appointments (all of that is deductible on your income taxes). Some of the other items to discuss include printing costs for promotional announcements, mailings, business cards, brochures, etc. Who covers the cost of signs and lock boxes? Some companies pay marketing costs like newspaper ads or to put your name on a bus bench. Others help with continuing education courses or special training classes.

Are there mandatory regular sales meetings and training programs? This will always be important to you, but it is critically helpful when you first enter the industry.

What type of personal training can I expect? If the sales manager is unavailable, are the other agents approachable as mentors? Some agents perceive you to be competition so they are not particularly helpful, but others are glad to help out. Don't be afraid to ask to meet the brokers who might be available to help you.

Are any leads provided? These may include referrals from agents of the same company, but out of the area. Sometimes, buyers call in because they see an ad in the paper for one of the office listings. Other buyers call because they see a sign on a property and they want to look at it. Sometimes, neighbors want to list their homes for sale and they just call the office closest to their home. And some people just walk in. Frequently, the sales manager and the veteran agents get most of these cherries, but there is probably some rotating schedule in place that can bring you some business from time to time.

Do I get any discounts or benefits if I buy or sell my own properties? One of the best benefits of having a license is that you have a jump start at lots of inventory. Profit dollars spend just as well as commission dollars so it is hoped you will pocket some of those dollars too.

Will you reimburse me for my schooling to get my license? That Learning Stool never stops giving. Here is a chance to get reimbursed for your schooling. You only get one chance to ask for this perk. Explain to the broker that you are looking at several offices and it would help you to make your decision if he would agree to reimburse you for your schooling out of the first commission check you generate. You might just get your money back. If not, at least he will know you are not afraid to ask for the order.

If we agree that I should work here, will you help me get familiar with the systems and procedures prior to my actually obtaining my license? In the weeks that follow you will be consumed with studying, but everybody needs a break now and then. During those moments you can begin doing things that will help you get a jump-start on your career. You can make client lists, attend sales meetings, inspect the new listings with other agents, attend training classes and go on appointments with agents in your new office.

You can send introductory letters to your clients. You may not tell them you already have a license but you can announce you are going to school to get your license and then send a follow-up letter announcing you passed the test. Many of your friends and potential clients will be pulling for you and they will enjoy being a part of your success.

Can you recognize how much further along you will be on your first day?

After you have finished this exercise with several brokers of interest, it should be fairly clear who has the best deal for you. Once you make your selection, Uncle Dave suggests you let all the brokers know what you decided, and why. Hopefully, you will be involved with them in future transactions and you want to have a first-class reputation with them.

Once that is accomplished, all that is left to do is go get your license.

Getting Your License

So far we have covered ten chapters of material before we have arrived at the point where it is time to discuss getting a license. There is a reason for that. Uncle Dave wanted you to appreciate just how much there is to know from that third leg of the Stool of Knowledge before you plunk down your hard-earned money at a real estate school.

> *It is possible for murderers and other felons to get a real estate license, but the financial crimes like embezzlement, fraud, money laundering and forgery are tougher to overcome because so much of the real estate transaction involves OPM (Other People's Money).*

Traditional real estate schools are the most common places

to accumulate the hours needed. These schools offer both online courses and actual classroom training. Their courses are reviewed and approved by the states for the purpose intended. The cost varies from a low of a few hundred dollars to $1,300 or so. Naturally, the ones that charge the most can usually justify why they think they are worth more. Some schools boast that 80% (or more) of their students pass the state exams the first time they take the test. For the students who don't pass, most of the schools offer follow-up training for cheap or free. Their goal is to help you pass the state exam and they are good at it.

These classes are not especially difficult but the volume of material is daunting (simple but not easy). The classes you take are considered college-level courses but don't let that scare you. If you still have good study skills you may do just fine studying online. However, if you are insecure about your study skills, I recommend you get your schooling right in the classroom. There is a temptation to do the opposite to avoid the risk of embarrassment, but the classroom setting is very friendly and you will be among others who are just as challenged as you are. I encourage you to pester the teacher. Ask questions. Stay after class and use this time for the purpose intended—to learn enough to pass the test the first time.

> *On their first day, many agents might as well take a bicycle with no handle bars to work because they don't know which way to turn.*

These schools do an effective job of teaching because they provide good materials and mock tests. Unlike in typical schools, mistakes are not held against you. Instead, they are used as a means to identify areas in which you need assistance. They have an excellent balance between teaching useful information and teaching directly to the test. In many cases they know exactly which questions you are likely to encounter on the exam, sometimes word for word. So, you will know the answers to many of the questions before you put your name on the test.

Your classes will likely include Real Estate Law, Practices of the Industry, Real Estate Math (not very tough), Closings, Contracts, Appraisal, Exam Preparation, and similar topics. Depending on the circumstances, you might be able to get through the required courses in as little as a few weeks, but it is not uncommon to take twice that long.

A few other points regarding licenses are worthy of mention. Many states allow for out-of-state licensees. Some states have reciprocating arrangements. For example, if you pass the test in California, other cooperating states may only require you to learn the issues that are peculiar to their state to obtain their license.

You should be advised that you will probably need to round up a set of fingerprints before the state actually issues your license. It can take a month for the authorities to do their background check and issue their report. So, you should consider getting that moving simultaneously with the start of your schooling so they will be ready by the time you pass the exam.

On their first day, many agents might as well take a bicycle with no handle bars to work because they don't know which way to turn; but if you employ the lessons of this chapter, you can hit the ground running. We know that time is always a limited commodity, but it is especially valuable in the early days. This chapter might just give you a two month head start on other licensees in your class. Good luck!

Before we jump to the next chapter, you should enjoy this tale, which illustrates just how important it can be to work in an office which is well matched to you.

Uncle Dave's True Story #11: King Poop and Peaches

One day, Kathy took advantage of Uncle Dave's reputation after she obtained a new listing from a family in search of a quick sale. The property may have been on King Street, but it was certainly not royalty. It lived in the middle of a lower-middle class neighborhood, only a few dozen feet from a very busy boulevard.

The owner was an elderly woman who had owned the home for a long time. Over all those years the property and the neighborhood came to become a little rough. Sadly, the aging woman eventually became vulnerable to thugs in the area. On several occasions the bad boys would visit the woman within a few days after she received her monthly Social Security check. Since she was relatively weak, it was easy to take her money. The police were called in but they never could put a stop to the problem. One month the lady tried to fight the intruders, but that was a big mistake. She was no match for them; that month, they beat her up before they stole her meager funds.

Fortunately, she had family members who allowed her to move in with them. However, they lived a few hundred miles away, so it took a while to gather her modest belongings. On one of their visits to her vacated home, they discovered a few homeless people were sneaking into the dwelling through a broken window to sleep at night. That was when the family realized they had to sell the little house. They called the police, boarded up the windows and turned off all the utilities including the water service. But those simple activities were not sufficient to discourage the uninvited guests from using the property to escape the cold.

Since the water was turned off, the toilet ran dry after a couple of flushes, but the uninvited occupants still needed a place to relieve themselves. After a week or so, there was a small mountain of waste in the unhappy stool.

By the time the family got around to marketing the home, things had gotten way out of hand. The police were making nightly inspections, but as soon as the cops would leave, the desperate intruders sneaked back in. The neighbors were irritated.

Several Realtors were contacted to inspect the potential listing, but they were so disgusted by all the flies and unsanitary conditions they didn't want to get involved. Besides, a small home like that would sell at such a low price, any potential commission would be insignificant. Who needs that?

Then Kathy got the call from the woman's family. Kathy had a soft spot for disadvantaged people so she told them she would see if she could get anybody who would take that home, at any price. I arrived at the home a few days later.

The middle of the day was a good time to visit, if there was such a thing, because the nightly visitors were nowhere to be seen. The stench was evident when I took my first step onto the rickety old porch. When I opened the front door, there were dozens of friendly flies who were anxious to greet me. The powerful stink was clear evidence why everybody else avoided this home. I forced myself to complete an inspection anyway.

The living room was ordinary in every way. Then, I peeked in the only bedroom and noticed the closet was tiny but otherwise the room was okay. Things got worse after that.

It did not take long to discover the source of the disgusting odor. I wanted to close the door to the bathroom but I forced myself to examine the rest of the room. I swatted hundreds of flies as I observed the little room had been remodeled about 15 years earlier. It was dated but in fairly good shape.

The kitchen counter was falling apart, the linoleum had outlived its useful life by ten years and the appliances looked like the type you see on old *I Love Lucy* reruns. I went down some steep, scary stairs into the compact and damp cellar. The old dirt floor was soggy with several inches of what I hoped was just mud. Then I noticed dozens of jars of canned peaches, which were stuffed into the floor joists overhead. Some of the fruit was so old it had turned black. What a mess.

When I returned upstairs, I noticed a small paint-starved door leading to an enclosed back porch. I realized the old door lent me an escape hatch to some fresh air for a moment or two. A quick inventory of the back yard revealed a tired and rotting fiberboard storage-shed that wanted to fall over. I walked toward it and discovered it was abuzz with an energetic swarm of hornets. There was no need to investigate it any closer. I knew I had to go back through the home to close it up. Before I did that, I observed that one section of the fence was falling over, the bushes were overgrown and the roof looked fairly good. I could not stall any longer. As I opened the back door and reentered the home, I observed something exciting: Hidden somewhere under the stench of human waste, I smelled something very pleasant. It was the sweet aroma of an awaiting profit.

I advised my co-worker of my findings. I explained the home was in decent shape for its age but it needed a lot of work and the cleanup was going to be most unpleasant. I explained that I could perform all that work and still make a fair profit provided I paid no more than thirty thousand dollars for the opportunity. The family was shocked that anybody would pay that much, so the deal closed a couple weeks later.

I usually send a maintenance crew to projects like that, but this property had special problems, so I knew I had to be there for the first day. We opened all the windows and hung fly strips around the home. It would take several more days before they were gone.

We turned the water back on and immediately discovered an innocent leak in a water pipe. That leak proved that the "mud" in the cellar was nothing more than that. After repairing the pipe, I got a hose and ran a very slow trickle of water into the toilet. It took me about twenty minutes to break through the mess and get the ceramic receptacle operating again.

Then, I put on a sweatshirt and visited the old shed in the back yard. When I opened the rickety door, the hornets made it perfectly clear that I was not welcome. I tried to ignore them as I sprayed their nest with a can of poison. Then several fought back. I was stung twice. Those little buzzers meant business. Later on, a couple of the maintenance crew members had the same unpleasant experience.

Finally, I went down into the cellar to get those peaches out of there. By the time it was over, I ventured up and down that squeaky little stairway dozens of times and pulled out more than 300 jars of canned peaches, some of them in antique bottles. A few jars were so fragile they could not support their own weight. They broke and made a stinky mess. Another group had been in jars so long they just dried up. And there were the black ones. I put all the jars on the floor of the back porch then we hauled them away. After that, the crew went to work and it wasn't long before the cozy little home was rented.

I recovered all my money by the end of the fifth year. After that, I enjoyed $600 a month in rent for another six years, for a total cash flow of more than $40,000. By then, the market improved and I sold the little home for $99,000. In the end, the house on King Street proved to be an excellent low-risk investment. Certainly $140,000 is worthy compensation for messing around with peaches, poop and hornets for a half-day.

Think about it. What did you learn?

Hint: Consider the perspectives of all of the agents.

Go to page 222 for your Instant Experience.

Chapter 12 – THE STATUS QUO IS NO WAY TO GO
or
Getting Better Is Better

Naturally, all new agents hope to put a couple of quick deals together to create a little financial breathing room. That is understandable because we cannot arrive in a theoretical future if we don't first survive each real day. But chasing individual transactions should be strictly a short-term strategy.

One excellent philosophy that will help you get out of the early hit-and-miss rut is to establish your long-term goals, and then make your day-to-day decisions based on how they help you accomplish those goals. When you know exactly what you are trying to do, every action and effort fits in somewhere.

> *Establish your long-term goals, and then make your day-to-day decisions based on how they help you accomplish those goals.*

Some of your long-term objectives should be to develop a first-rate image, to expand your pool of knowledge and to put back into the industry.

These things take time, effort and money, but do not overlook them for long because they are essential in your quest to move from the ranks of new licensees to being an accomplished, permanent professional. Once you catch your breath, here are the important things that demand your attention.

BUILDING YOUR IMAGE

My daddy (I guess he would be your great-uncle) once told me, "Take care of your reputation; it is your most valuable asset." That was good advice. Long-term success is much easier for individuals who exhibit character traits like that. Along those lines, one of the wisest things you can do is establish a good image of yourself. You will be judged based on your physical impression and how you interact with other persons. The good news is you can begin that process immediately.

Physical Impressions

There was a time when dressing "professionally" meant suits and ties for men and skirts, dresses or pantsuits for women; but there is much more flexibility now.

> *Some people will love to swill a few beers and discuss the virtues of a $20 cigar with you.*

How You Look

Some brokers expend a great deal of effort in a quest to make a specific visual impression. One agent always wore classy two-tone custom-made shoes. A lady Realtor had a strong connection to breast cancer issues so she always wore a tasteful pink ribbon to show her concern. A Texan moved out of state, then went to great lengths to exaggerate his heritage (big ol' hats and a deep southern drawl are unique in these-here parts, pardner); his individuality has served him extremely well. You could be known for odd neckties, flamboyant hats or being the lady who shaves her head if you think that will help you.

Regardless of how you choose to present yourself, you must consider the consequences of your choices. Overly creative wardrobes might offend the proper folks and the suit and tie may seem intimidating or arrogant to young, first-time buyers. If you are a member of the tattoo and piercing crowd, there will be individuals who like that, but be advised that unorthodox images reduce your range of appeal.

Do you really want to risk offending prospective clients?

Your Transportation

Once upon a time the Cadillac was the symbol of success, but nowadays there are plenty of high-quality vehicles. If you plan on driving a vehicle like that, there are a couple things to think about. First, some of us believe that a new Mercedes (or any other super luxury vehicle) only impresses other Mercedes owners. If you plan on specializing in upscale properties, such a vehicle may be perfect for you, but other people think it is a sign that you make too much money—their money.

One successful broker I know did so well for such a long time, he eventually focused most of his efforts on working with sellers. Since he basically stopped hauling buyers around, he bought a cute little two-seater Porsche convertible and it never hurt him a bit.

A lot of my business in the early years came from first-time buyers and entry-level investors, so I drove a nice but modest four-door, gas-guzzling Ford. In today's climate, Uncle Dave suggests an SUV that is two to four years old and can serve both as family transportation and a useful work vehicle. A car like that is practical, affordable and non-objectionable.

In this new era of "green" mentality, there are customers

167

who appreciate agents who drive hybrids or electric cars. In some of the busiest cities some agents can even make a great living without even owning a car. It is possible to make a living selling real estate whether you ride a dump-truck, a bicycle or a classic car. Just remember that whatever you choose establishes an image, especially, in the eyes of people who don't know you very well.

Other Visual Issues

There are additional things to consider when you are building an image via a visual presentation. Your hair, clothes, jewelry, make-up, tennis shoes and everything else plays a role. If you drink or smoke, people will judge you for those habits. Some people will love to swill a few beers and discuss the virtues of a $20 cigar with you, but others have seen family members suffer horrible fates because of those "vices." Keep these things in mind whenever you go out in public because you never know who you might meet. Remember the old cliché: You only get one chance to make a good first impression.

How You Interact with Others

Very few brokers would have gotten a comment on a report card that said, "does not get along with others." The real estate industry is a people business. If you like working with the public you will probably fit in naturally, but here are a few things to consider.

How You Behave

One broker I know has the excellent quality of remaining calm in the face of problems. That serves him well most of the time because it enables him to remain focused on solutions rather than some of the less fruitful choices, but there is a flip side to this coin. I have heard one of his clients wonder if the broker really cares what happens to the client. Another broker I know is nearly the opposite. Whenever he walks in a room he is so filled with enthusiasm he perks some people right up. But I have also heard him referred to as a glad-hander, which was to suggest his motives were insincere and his happy face was nothing more than a means of self-promotion.

Regardless of how you behave, you are not going to please everybody, but try to temper any extreme behavioral tendencies that might offend other people.'

Relationships with Clients

These people are much more than a means to an end. Donna has been a top producer since the '70s. She works in a small mountain town, mostly with locals and people in the second-home market. She has an excellent reputation, so I asked her about her success. She said, "I really care about my people and their families." She went on to tell me, "I never worry about the money. I know it will be there. I just want to be certain they get what they need and want." I could sense her compassion and I am certain it earns loyalty, repeat business and referrals from her clients. This successful professional reaps big rewards because of the value she places on building high-quality relationships with her clients, rather than the money they represent.

> *Uncle Dave and Patty once took twelve people from a property management company to Las Vegas. We paid for the airfare and hotel rooms in one of the luxury casinos. It cost us more than $5,000, but those people were very committed to renting up our vacant units. One occupied apartment paid us $7,000 per year, and they rented many dozen of them for us every year. Their services were priceless to us. They certainly deserved to know we were grateful.*

> *Uncle Dave has also provided transportation and a luxury condominium on the beach near San Diego to the families of title representatives, mortgage lenders, personal assistants, coworkers, and maintenance people. Can you imagine how much these people appreciate the memories they created with their children?*

Relationships with Fellow Agents

If you hang around long enough, you will come in contact with the successful agents on repeated occasions. These people may be competitors, but they are not enemies. Therefore, they are very important to your success. When you call them with feedback regarding their listing or send them an unexpected thank you note following a successful transaction you gain their notice and earn their respect. When you reach out in those ways, your seemingly insignificant gestures pay handsome dividends.

On some occasions, Uncle Dave has received multiple offers on certain listings. If I already had a good relationship with one of the brokers involved, I certainly let my client know. There have been times when that past relationship determined whose contract was accepted.

Relationships with Support Personnel

Have you ever worked for somebody who genuinely valued you as a person? If so, you probably would have run through a brick wall for that person. Agents are a lot like bosses. There are all sorts of people whose jobs depend on us, such as receptionists, administrators and personal assistants. We also need a gang of other helpers such as title representatives, lenders and appraisers. These people are a blessing to you. Why treat them otherwise? Uncle Dave suggests you worship at the altar of their feet.

Take them to lunch once in a while. If they worked especially hard for you, buy them a gift certificate to take their family out to dinner. If they are reliable, professional, or especially ethical let them know you notice it. Treat them like they matter to you and they will treat you like you matter to them. Licensees who understand the value of their associates have a much better opportunity of succeeding in the long term. Now you are one of those wiser brokers.

Any worthwhile relationship requires a little effort. Your image is like that. To enhance your professional life, you need to pay attention to your image and work on it regularly.

PERPETUAL TRAINING

Uncle Dave has been licensed for 30 years. I have sold hundreds of homes and thousands of apartments. I have hosted a real estate call-in radio program, written newspaper articles and taught classes both to the public and other real estate offices. I have owned and operated my own real estate company and a property management company. I have sub-divided land and converted apartments into condominiums. I have owned hundreds of rental properties. I have bought tax certificates and countless foreclosure properties. I have attended hundreds of meetings, seminars and training classes. And guess what. I still love to learn new things.

Uncle Dave has a PhD diploma from Harvard Business School, majoring in real estate. I sometimes pass it around the room whenever I am invited to speak. It lends me great credibility. Later in the evening, after I have shared my information on financial planning, working with investors or investing, I confess that I bought the diploma on eBay for under $10. The attendees get a kick out of that because they are completely taken in by the gag.

> *I believe that these students are a lot like me. They love to learn new things and they don't particularly care if the information comes from a great book, a seminar or a person with a PhD (legitimate or not). When it comes to learning, the source is much less important than the knowledge gained.*

This week I visited a new golfing community in the mountains, just to learn about it. The point is, even though I already know a substantial amount about real estate, I constantly seek to learn new information. You should too.

WHY KEEP LEARNING?

Reclaim Your Time

In an early chapter we identified enough time as one of the Top Ten tools you need in this industry. In a paradoxical way, the more time you invest in learning new things the more time off you will have. I am sure you have heard the old saying, "work smarter, not harder." That is the essence of knowledge. The more you learn, the easier life becomes. When you start out, you will need help with everything, but as you gain experience you can do the same job in less time. That is called a learning curve. It is certainly worth your time to continue learning.

Make More Money

The more you know the more chances you have to increase your income. The broader and deeper your knowledge, the more valuable you become. More money usually means a better quality of life, but better still, the more money you have to invest and build your passive income, the sooner your retirement train will arrive.

Prestige

One of the many reasons to continue taking classes and growing your knowledge is you will gain great respect from your new-found wisdom. Structured learning is not a substitute for experience but it is a great way to gather information and professional designations—you know… all those capital letters behind our names. With those designations comes a feeling of accomplishment and implied credibility.

See www.realtor.org/education/realtor_university/designations for all of the options.

HOW TO DO IT

Continuing Education Courses

These classes are required to keep your license current. In our state there is an eight-hour mandatory class, once every three years. In addition, the licensee has to collect another 16 hours from any combination of a wide menu of choices. Other states have similar requirements. Contact your state's licensing authority.

Seminars

Seminars can be inspiring and informative. Sometimes, top sales people and other experts are retained by real estate companies. These speakers are among the best in the field and they can be very inspirational. Go learn from them.

Still other seminars are offered by escrow companies, lenders, Associations of Realtors and traditional real estate schools. Some of them offer continuing education credits. Most of them are informative and worth your time.

Conventions

Okay, you party animals, this one's for you. Our state and other ones have an annual Realtor Rally that attracts thousands of licensees for the purpose of socializing, learning and motivating. There are plenty of folks who never miss this event. There are guest speakers, promotional booths, and lots of experts at your fingertips. Some brokers travel quite a distance and make a big slumber party out of it. There is plenty to gain by attending these events. These programs offer great opportunities to enjoy your peers and build important relationships.

On a grander scale, the National Association of Realtors sponsors an annual three-day Conference and Expo each fall. It is in a different city each year. There are famous speakers from the sports world, Hollywood and business circles. All the latest issues are explored, including new legislative topics, marketing techniques, new construction trends, tenant/landlord topics, senior housing, exciting new tools, technology updates, second home markets and much more. These offer a fantastic mini-vacation and you probably can deduct most of the expenses.

JOKE TIME - One not-too-bright real estate agent had a lot of miles on her Lexus so she was trying to sell it, but she could not find any takers. When she complained of the problem to her sales manager he asked her how many miles were on it. The agent confessed that it had already traveled nearly 300,000 miles. "Well, no wonder," scoffed the sales manager. "You need to do something drastic." So he told her about a friend who would turn the odometer back for her, but she would have to "keep it quiet" because it was illegal. Relieved at the prospect of any solution she decided she would gladly do that. A month later the not-too-bright agent was still driving that same car and the sales manager asked why she hadn't sold it. She said, "You must be nuts; why would I want to sell a car that only has 45,000 miles on it?"

Fun Around the Neighborhood

There is plenty of training and knowledge to pick up right in your own back yard. Many communities offer an annual Parade of Homes wherein several builders construct mini-palaces and open them for viewing. Other new subdivisions will welcome your visits. And then there are local trade shows and home and garden shows in the shopping malls. We recently visited a show that was just about log homes. It was very interesting. Anytime you visit these places you pick up new information. Who said learning has to be boring?

On Your Own

The most reliable way to gain knowledge and training is on your own. You can learn at your own pace and anytime you wish. Once you get into the self-teaching mode, you become a magnet and there is a world of information to serve as your iron scraps. Let's explore the worthy ways you can get smarter on your own.

Experience

The very best source of knowledge is the School of Hard Knocks. You will learn more from your own successes and failures than anything else because the training is 100 percent relevant to you. If a seminar speaker tells you why you need to get a seller to sign a listing agreement as soon as possible, you will "intellectually" understand what is meant. But if your brother lists his home with another broker because he thought you only work on the other side of town, you will "feel" the same message all the way to the deepest recesses of your broken heart.

Books

I won't belabor the obvious benefits of reading books (including this one) but I might suggest you are too nice to your books. I write all over my books. Underlining is for wimps. I make bold circles around worthy paragraphs; I scribble comments all over the pages. I make follow-up notes on the Table of Contents page to remind me which chapters were special. The next time I grab that same book I can quickly scan the pages and essentially speed-read it, thereby keeping the germane points in my thoughts. All that priceless information costs only a few bucks per book. What a bargain.

Audio CDs

My son drives about 20,000 miles per year. He leads an active life and rarely has the time to curl up with books, but he still likes the mental stimulation of learning new things. CDs provide the perfect solution. He has studied all sorts of specialty topics on his own and has found an efficient way to exploit his situation. One good source for real estate related CDs is www. realestatebooks.org.

From Your TV

There are many television programs offering knowledge and training. A quick look through my own satellite system reveals shows like *Holmes on Homes, Flip This House, Moving Up, House Hunters, Designed to Sell, Secrets That Sell, Curb Appeal* and *My House Is Worth What?* Some of them are catchy because they have a soap opera flair. A new licensee can learn a lot about the selling process and the psychology of the transaction right from the proverbial idiot box.

From Your Peers

Uncle Dave really likes this technique. One of the best ways to self-train is to piggyback on your peers. Go with them on a listing presentation or invite them to join you when you visit with a buyer. Then tell each other what you learned. Pick their brains, constantly. Here are a few examples of the ways Uncle Dave has done that.

- When I hosted my radio program, I frequently invited a wide variety of peers to each act as my co-host for a day. Uncle Dave picked their brains right on the air, constantly learning how they approached the business.
- Duane and I went on several appointments together. There was an occasion when I was considering the purchase or a rental property but I hesitated because the asking price was way too high, so I assumed the seller was unrealistic. Aware of my angst, Duane asked me an unusually simple question, "Would you pay a dollar?"

  No deep thought was necessary so I snidely shot back the obvious answer, "Of course." Before I caught my breath, he modified the question and asked it again, "Would you pay a thousand dollars?" I did not know what he was getting at, but I affirmed my previous response. Then he drove his point home, "Well obviously, you like the property and you would pay something, but not the amount the seller is asking. You never know what a seller will accept so why don't you make your best offer and see what happens?"

  What a fantastic way to encourage an apprehensive buyer to make an offer. I have employed his idea plenty of times to encourage buyers to make offers for properties that they believed were out of their reach.

  To this day, I still use the concept on myself. Occasionally, I get a great deal on a property I nearly overlooked. One seller accepted an offer that was 24% below the asking price. Thank you, Duane.

- I already had ten years of experience when I went on a listing appointment with Al just to learn how this seasoned professional worked. He had a particularly effective way of discussing how to price the home which I copied thereafter.

When Al discussed pricing with a potential seller, he said something like this, "We need to price it low enough to create excitement, but not so low that we leave any of your money on the table." The sellers nodded their heads in approval and Al got another well priced listing.

In life, a baby crawls before it walks. The same is true for the licensee who is determined to succeed. Once you have the basics under your feet, it is time to broaden your education for all of the reasons mentioned above. You can do that by rubbing elbows with your peers or curling up with a book or any number of other ways. But the person who is not constantly learning new things is stuck in a rut and flirting with mediocrity… or worse.

GIVING BACK

One of the reasons The Association of Realtors and the entire industry is so powerful is because of thousands of unselfish professionals who came before you. Most of these people devoted their precious time to the advancement of the concepts we embrace. Once you gather a little momentum, you should begin to seek out ways that you can also "give back." You can do that through the Realtor Association or directly into the community.

Through the Realtor Associations

Your local, state and national associations all need you. There are many committees and activities waiting for your efforts. Uncle Dave served on the Grievance Committee but there are many others. Some of those include Political Action, Membership, Finances, Education, Community Service, Awards, Special Projects, Professional Standards and more. There also has to be a governing body, which includes the board members and the president of each association. Some of these positions require a great deal of time but they can be very fulfilling.

Your local association will also have interesting activities in which you might want to participate. Our association recruits helpers to clean up and paint the home of one elderly person each year. You can expect to find events like pancake breakfasts to raise funds for needy causes, blood drives, marches for worthwhile causes, assistance for citizens with diseases such as Muscular Dystrophy and whatever else comes up.

The Realtor Association is a very worthwhile organization, which is deeply devoted to promoting its members, the community and the underlying purpose of our professional existence: helping others with their housing needs. Once you are able to give back, your contributions will be most welcomed. Please allow Uncle Dave to be the first person to thank you for your kind deeds in that regard.

In the Community

There are plenty of ways you can help the community. Uncle Dave suggests the causes that hold some relationship to housing. For example, I have served on a committee that caters to the needs of single parents. Essentially, their apartments are provided at about 30% of market rents and day care is free to help approved candidates get on their feet. Volunteers help with a lot of the activities and other people make financial contributions. One time we bought 500 pairs of blue jeans and donated them to the community. We have also provided a lot of the decorations for Halloween and Christmas.

We also like to provide food and essentials for a homeless shelter in our city. It seems to me that somebody who has enjoyed so many blessings from the housing industry ought to be able to help the people who do not have a place to call home.

There are many other worthwhile ways you can give back within the community. You can sponsor a cleanup section along the highway and even get your name on a sign which reminds people of your commitment. Most big cities have government organizations that assist less fortunate citizens to upgrade their homes. Volunteers are needed to install caulking, add insulation, secure doors and similar activities.

I am sure you have heard of the organization known as Habitat for Humanity, but have you ever considered joining them in their cause (if interested, check out www.habitat.org)? You could help the families of sick children by contributing time or funds to the Ronald McDonald House Charities (visit www. MHC.com for one near you). And, of course, you could speak with the leaders of your church to discuss ways your donations can be used to promote housing issues, such as hiring somebody to mow the lawn of a senior, or helping somebody pay their rent or utility fees.

Naturally, your efforts do not have to be tied to real estate issues. One husband/wife team I know devotes a great deal of time taking disabled children to the ski slopes. Other brokers increase their activities within their churches. When it comes to "giving back" in the community, the options are plentiful. You might be amazed at all the ways your successful peers do this. Uncle Dave hopes you will quickly gain success and enjoy the same great feelings we experience as we help others fulfill their dreams.

Becoming a true professional is like many other topics within this book and life itself. It is simple to say, but it is not particularly easy to do. As you advance through your career, Uncle Dave hopes you will always strive to get better by constantly Building

Your Image, pursuing Perpetual Training and finding ways to Give Back. Then you will be complete.

The following story will introduce you to one special broker friend who has always represented our industry in these ways.

Uncle Dave's True Story #12: The Smoke House

There was a young family with two young daughters which bought a home in a western suburb of Denver. The mom was an excellent seamstress who accumulated hundreds of bolts of fabric and patterns to make all sorts of clothes, especially dresses. She had a fantastic sewing shop with commercial grade machines set up in the lower level of their home.

Unfortunately, life was not good for the two young girls. I never heard exactly what the problem was but by the time I met the younger sister, she was in her thirties and quite a tragic story.

Keith was a soft-spoken and especially decent broker who worked in our office. One day he stopped by my office for a talk. He had just taken a listing and he thought I was the right buyer for it. A recent fire had damaged the home. There were losses from smoke, water and fire. The seller was the younger sister mentioned earlier. The home was the one in which she was raised.

Her father had died years earlier and her mom had passed on more recently. The older sister had gotten married and started her own family somewhere out of state. That left one lonely woman who was still single living in a home that was way too big for her and filled with sad memories of a childhood gone by. She tried to fill the emptiness in her life with a large collection of dogs and cats.

One day, the young woman decided that maintaining that home and living there was more than she could tolerate. Most owners would call a Realtor, but she was so distraught she took a more ominous route. First she put all of her pets in one of the bedrooms. Then, she found a can of charcoal lighter fluid and squirted it all over the living room carpet and drapes. After she started the fire, she retreated to the bedroom with the only friends she cared about and waited for the inevitable outcome.

The blaze quickly consumed the curtains and filled the home with smoke. The heat built up to a point where one of the windows exploded. Fortunately, one of the neighbors heard the racket and called the fire department. By the time they finished their work they chopped a hole in the roof, drowned the living room in water, and left an enormous mess. They made a final sweep of the house and then they found the owner crouched in the corner, huddling with all her four-legged friends. Fortunately, they all survived.

Somebody told Keith of the circumstances and he was the perfect agent to talk with the young woman. This situation was not about money to him. It was about serving somebody who needed his help. He turned everything around for her. He advised her that he knew a guy (me) who might take her home just like it was, plus pay off her loan and all her expenses and give her $10,000 to get a fresh start somewhere else. He gave her hope and suddenly she decided life would be worth living, after all. The entire concept was a deep relief for her. Keith brought the deal to me because he knew that I would also appreciate her circumstances.

When we wrote the contract, we told her she did not have to leave anything behind which she wanted to take with her and she did not have to take anything she wanted to leave. I agreed to clean up the entire mess, regardless of what that might be. When I took possession, I was surprised by how little she wanted. In addition to the items that could not be salvaged, she left behind all the family photo albums, all the pictures on the walls and other things that seemed like typical family mementoes. She wanted nothing to do with the sewing room or anything in it.

We donated the machines along with any other useful items to a charity. We gave away some of the material to anybody who wanted it. We did not know anybody who had a use for the patterns (eBay was not around) so we threw them out—hundreds of them.

It took several days and a couple of construction dumpsters to get rid of a lifetime of belongings and so many bad memories.

Once the property was gutted down to the walls we began to put it back together. Then one day, the seller returned. She was cheerful and wanted a favor. She asked us for two of the large rocks that were part of the landscaping. They had to weigh 200 pounds each. We had no obligation to give them to her, but there was no reason to deny her this irrelevant request. The next Monday when the crew showed up to work at the home, the rocks were gone. I don't know what was so special about them, but I hoped they brought her some sort of pleasure. Some years later, Keith told me she was happily working in an animal hospital.

When the work was completed, the home still had a slight smoky smell. But we were able to sell it anyway and recover all our money and a modest profit, a profit I would have gladly forfeited if the distressed woman would have sold her home before she got to a point where she felt a fire was her best option.

Think about it. What did you learn?

Hint: Consider Keith's role.

Go to page 223 for your Instant Experience.

Chapter 13 – TINKER WITH YOUR THINKER
or
Jobs of the Industry

Perhaps you still like the idea of getting a sales license, but you would like to learn some of the less traditional positions or how you might phase into the business. In the latter case, you might find one of the salaried jobs of this chapter to your liking. If you are more convinced than ever that the world of real estate sales is the correct course for you, it is still prudent to understand the role of the remaining cast members.

LICENSED POSITIONS

Property Managers

This profession is not especially glamorous but it might surprise the reader to learn that a lot of property managers become millionaires. Some of them specialize in leasing and managing commercial properties including retail centers, office buildings and warehouses but there are also plenty of positions in residential properties. Some of those include rental houses, condominiums, apartment buildings, Home Owner Associations, senior communities and vacation rental properties. This career alternative offers the broker several streams of income. We will discuss a typical residential property management situation.

Suppose a small company manages 300 apartment units and 200 single family homes. Let's examine what the broker might expect. Residential property managers usually charge the owner of the property a percentage of rents collected. This is a fabulous base income. If each one of the units rents for $650 per month, and the property manager charges 6% of the collected rent that amounts to a respectable automatic income of nearly $20,000 per month.

In addition, there is frequently a rent-up fee when a vacant home or condominium is rented. It is not uncommon for the manager to earn half of the first month's rent for this service. Using the numbers mentioned above, the manager can expect around $4,000 dollars per month in additional income from this effort. He or she does not usually receive compensation when apartment units are rented because the on-site manager usually performs that duty.

JOKE TIME - Two women were jogging down the street when they came upon an open house. They went inside to look around and eventually went out to the back porch. Suddenly a frog jumped up on the table and said to them, "Please help me. I am a real estate agent and I got caught lying, so a witch turned me into a frog. But, if one of you will kiss me, I can be a real estate agent again."

One of the women quickly grabbed the frog and stuffed it into her fanny pack. The other woman was surprised and said, "Hey, didn't you hear him say if we kissed him he could become a real estate agent again?"

"Yeah, I know, but a talking frog has got be worth a lot more than a real estate agent."

Property managers are also known to share in any late fees that are collected from slow-paying tenants. The manager has to fill out notices, as well as deliver and post them at the property, plus work with the court system to enforce the lease terms. This extra time and effort justifies extra income. That will generate an additional $2,000 each month for the manager. But we are not done yet.

These professionals frequently get early notice that their owner/clients intend to sell their rental properties, so the manager has an opportunity to list that property for sale or earn a referral fee for sending it to a qualified sales agent. If the owner is especially motivated, our management friends are frequently positioned to buy the property themselves, perhaps locking in enormous profits. It would not be difficult to land another $4,000 per year from this source. But wait, there is still more.

Most of the better tenants have aspirations of buying their own home, so the property manager has a fantastic inside track to all these first-time buyers, or anybody else a tenant might refer to the manager for that purpose. Obviously, there is potential to irritate an owner if you encourage tenants to move out, so this situation has to be handled carefully, and with full disclosure. My property manager shares some of the commission he earns when he sells a property to one of my tenants. I understand that some tenants end up buying homes and I am going to lose some of them anyway, so why not get a little bit out of the relationship? This income stream can easily be another $10,000 per year for the manager.

The property manager enjoys some other benefits in addition to multiple streams of income. One of the fantastic ones is they are insulated from most seasonal issues or other market problems caused by struggling economies. In the winter months, when sales slow down for residential brokers, the renters like to stay put. That protects the income of our property management friends. Similar benefits are enjoyed when the residential sales market slows down due to high interest rates or any other causes.

In disastrous times the manager still has great opportunities. If one of the apartment buildings suddenly has a 25% vacancy rate, the owner could be on the verge of bankruptcy but the property manager still pulls his or her income right off the top of the remaining occupied apartments. Furthermore, if owners lose their properties in times like that, the foreclosing banks still need the property managers to generate as much income as possible.

So, what about the overhead? The manager needs several helpers to get the job done. There needs to be a receptionist, a bookkeeper and an assistant or two to show vacant units and coordinate repairs. There are also a few office expenses like rent payments, utilities, insurance payroll taxes and other typical costs. All of this overhead will devour approximately half of the total income.

Therefore, after taking in the revenues and paying all the expenses, our manger friends can expect to earn between $150,000-$250,000 per year for a portfolio of this size. Not bad, especially considering the stability factor.

Obviously, the new licensee cannot usually start out with 500 units but he or she can go to work for somebody else who has a corral full of inventory. Chances are you can get a salary for helping with the management duties and perhaps make extra commission dollars renting vacant units and selling homes to the tenants.

If residential property management appeals to you, Uncle Dave recommends you look for a firm that is great at customer service, or great at prospecting for new business (although very few of them do this well). If possible, work for one of these companies for a year or two, and then shift to the other style of company for a similar period.

During this self-directed apprenticeship, you are attempting to learn how to attract business from one of the firms and how to keep it from the other one. You will also learn other skills such as showing apartments, dealing with tenants, coordinating repairs and similar things. Once you have a sufficient background to understand how to get business and how to keep it, you should be ready to start your own company.

Once you arrive at that point, you can get business by buying out other companies. Or, you can drop by apartment buildings to offer your services. You can obtain the owner's contact information and ask them for their business. You can contact brokers who sell apartment buildings then approach the new owners after a sale is completed. You can also visit the county records to learn about any other transfers that have taken place. Finally, you can designate one of your employees to call private parties who advertise their rental homes in the newspaper or on Craigslist to see if those owners have ever considered the advantages of hiring a manager.

The commercial property management positions offer similar benefits: steady income, rent-up fees, and early access to inventory for listings or your own investments. With so many powerful income streams, is it any wonder these quiet workers frequently rake in the big bucks?

One of my colleagues was a very conservative fellow named Howard. He started out as a property manager working for a salary at one of the bigger firms in Denver. Eventually, he decided he knew enough to go out on his own. He sent letters to everybody he could think of announcing his new company and asking for business. He even sent announcements to people and places which the bigger firms ignored.

Things started out slowly for Howard. Then one day he received a frantic call from a bank officer who received one of those letters. Earlier, the bank had financed the construction of a mid-sized residential community, consisting of approximately 100 modest single-family homes. Apparently, the contractor was having difficulty selling his inventory so he rented out most of the homes to generate some income. To compound matters, he was not a very successful property manager either, so the bank foreclosed on the properties.

Right away the bank officers got bombarded with calls from disgruntled tenants. There were broken hot water heaters, vacant homes and damaged yards. Some tenants were moving out, and other prospective tenants wanted to see the homes that were available to rent. Plumbers, carpet installers and other workers were needed right away. The bank officers immediately realized they were in over their heads and needed professional help. Then they got Howard's letter. We can only wonder who was more excited to meet the other: Howard or the bank officers.

A meeting ensued and it wasn't long before Howard was confronted with the surprise of a lifetime. He thought they wanted him to take over management of the community but they had different plans. Instead, they wanted him to BUY the entire project. Well, as I stated earlier Howard was ultra-conservative and he had a very young family to look after. He was also newly self-employed, so he didn't have many accounts or very much income. He knew he had no business taking on such an enormous project. I imagine he was disappointed that the bank's goals did not match his own.

But the bank was motivated—VERY, VERY MOTIVATED. They told Howard to buy the properties in the name of a corporation, so he wouldn't have to put his own name on the deal. They agreed to finance the entire purchase, with no down payment. They gave him an interest rate to drool over. They agreed to let him collect rents for a while before making his first payment, so he could build up some operating capital. They agreed to let him sell individual properties to generate extra capital whenever he needed it. And, they offered the properties to him at below market prices, so he would be virtually guaranteed to make a nice profit. The whole deal seemed too good to be true so Howard raced over to his attorney to find out if he had overlooked something. Soon, he realized he had won his own personal lottery.

Over the next dozen years he sold off about one-third of the properties. But then the flood gates opened. The market prices of those homes doubled and redoubled, then did it again. Rents also went up and naturally Howard landed plenty of other accounts over the years. That is when I met him. By that time, he had a sales department for the benefit of his investor-clients as well as the tenants who were ready to buy homes. Howard invited Uncle Dave to join that department. That was my first licensed position.

Howard employed lots of people over the years and he never let his success go to his head. This humble man always treated everybody with respect. His fine example was an inspiration to me and many others.

Howard's story is special but it is not unique. Your trusted uncle and many others have enjoyed similar benefits (but not usually that incredible) by associating with the property management side of the industry. It does not take a deal like the one that Howard found to change your life forever. That is why so many property managers are millionaires.

On-Site Sales

This is another great way to phase into the business. There are opportunities with tract homes, custom homes, time-share programs, vacant land sales and specialty projects like senior communities or recreational properties in places such as Las Vegas, ski towns or along the beach. Sometimes agents can get a salary-plus-bonus arrangement.

These positions are well suited to people who don't really

care for the "knocking on doors" part of traditional residential sales. You are not always expected to generate your own leads but you do have to convert prospects into buyers. In essence, you are like an auto, furniture or retail salesperson. When customers come to the "showroom" the broker attempts to sell one of the on-site products. In certain situations, the smart agent can turn this situation into a gold mine.

Simultaneously with the impending retirement of the baby boomers, luxurious golfing communities are sprouting up all over the place. The greens are surrounded like cul-de-sacs with second-home mini-mansions that would humble the primary residences of our great-grandparents. Opportunities abound for brokers who enjoy golfing and rubbing elbows with some of our more financially blessed citizens.

Some communities hire their own independent brokers but others hire outside agencies to represent them. There are a wide range of compensation packages, which can include salaries with bonuses or straight commission arrangements. Free golf is common, especially if the sales people are courting prospective customers. Some projects even provide housing for their sales people.

Brokers often get to meet interesting and successful people. Each course has a professional golfer on staff and most courses have both a male and female pro to promote their project.

Most of the developers help to generate leads via Internet Web sites, mailings and special promotions. In some cases, the agents are expected to generate their own leads, but the same outlets are pursued.

Many on-site agents are allowed to assist the owners to resell their properties when they elect to move out of the communities. Some brokers gain such an excellent reputation among the residents that when the community sells out the brokers transfer their licenses to a local resale office and continue to specialize in the community for many more years.

Similar opportunities are available selling time-share properties or town home communities in other recreational environments or retirement communities. If the reader finds this concept to be intriguing, it is recommended you visit some nearby projects to determine what opportunities are available.

A more typical way to use on-site sales to your benefit is found in traditional residential communities. Uncle Dave worked with Tom for nearly twenty years. Even though he went to college, it never played much of a role in his extraordinary success. As a young man, he accepted an on-site position selling several hundred modest tract homes. It took several years to sell out the subdivision and Tom made a nice income from his effort. But the greater benefit came from the fact that he met nearly all of the buyers of those homes.

A fair number of the people who bought those new homes used other brokers to assist them in the purchase. But amazingly, very few of those brokers did the type of things necessary to earn any repeat business from the clients. Naturally, Tom got most of that business, too.

All subdivisions have people who must move and that one was no different. Some of those people barely moved into their new homes before they became victims of job changes, divorces, corporate transfers or financial problems. Fortunately for Tom, nobody was better poised to seize that opportunity than he was. Everybody liked Tom and he knew the inventory better than anybody else did. That dynamic package opened doors to all those sellers. But there was more.

There was all the spin-off business. Some sellers move out of state and Tom picked up referral fees by finding good agents to help them buy new properties in their new destinations. Other sellers stayed in the general area and bought something new. Naturally, Tom harvested plenty of cherries off that tree, as well.

Then there is that little thing called customer service. Tom knew exactly how to take care of his clients and they sent bucketsful of referrals and most of them came back again and again. But Tom's story does not end there.

He surrounded himself with similarly dynamic brokers and eventually several of them joined forces to open a powerhouse RE/MAX franchise. That awesome company grew into several offices with well over a hundred brokers, each paying monthly fees for the privilege of working there. After more good years, Tom decided it was time to "give back," so he took on responsibilities at the local Association of Realtors. A year later he became president of the local chapter and the next year, he was elected President of the Colorado Association of Realtors. All of that started by one young fellow working on-site, selling homes in a modest subdivision. Tom's story is proof positive that on-site sales can provide a worthy income, especially in the beginning. But, it can also be a superb springboard to an incredible career, as he proved when he used that opportunity as the first rung on a professional ladder to excellence.

In the beginning of this book Uncle Dave pointed out an enigma. I suggested it is odd that so many average and normal people do extremely well in our business while many other equally gifted people never do figure it out. Howard and Tom were both humble people. They would both gladly admit that they were not extraordinary at all. Now that you know their stories, I hope you appreciate why I have spent so much time encouraging you.

Licensed Assistant

Another good phase-in position involves the new licensee aligning with another successful broker who has too many customers to work effectively. The leader shares good leads with the helper and they split the commission dollars generated by their joint efforts. The split is open to negotiation but it would be reasonable for the helper to get 50-60% and the leader to take the remainder.

The trick here is to be certain your leader really has a steady stream of hot leads for you. One agent I knew was always a top producer but he worked way too many hours. From time to time he would realize he was missing important family events and decide to hire a licensed assistant. Things usually worked out for a couple of months before the same old problem would return.

The assistants were less effective than he was, which frustrated him. Rather than teach the helpers how to be more effective, he responded by keeping all of the better leads even if that meant he had to work them himself. Once the quality of their leads diminished, the assistants grew frustrated. Eventually, they had to look for a different job and several months later the cycle would repeat itself. The licensed helpers could have saved themselves some problems if they would have investigated this fellow better.

Do not be discouraged by the above example because there are many other brokers who are more stable. For instance, Jace is such an incredible producer that he has two full-time assistants and he considers it his duty to help them both make a six-figure income.

The agent who is interested in this type of work can send brochures to hundreds of agents offering to perform this service. Simply call a good real estate office in your area and ask them if there are any brochure-delivery services in the area (if there are no such services, tell somebody you know to open a company that delivers brochures to all of the Realtors in your community). It may take several such distributions but at 10 cents for each delivered brochure, the cost is modest. Another option is to place an ad in the publications of the local Associations of Realtors. The bottom line is, if you can find the right leader, you can make their job easier or increase their income, and that makes you valuable.

Once you find someone with whom you want to work, ask for permission to talk with some of the other agents in the office who know your potential leader. Then try to find out if the leader is likely to have worthwhile leads for you on an ongoing basis. If you find the right fit, you have a great way to serve your apprenticeship.

The Specialists

There are several other licensed possibilities, but they are generally too sophisticated for entry-level agents to consider. However, they are mentioned here to introduce the reader to less familiar options. These positions do not ordinarily offer salaries.

- Auctioneer - A great way to guarantee a sale
- Business broker - Sells businesses with or without buildings
- Commercial broker - Leases or sells offices, retail centers, industrial facilities, land for development or apartment buildings
- Project manager – Contact commercial companies; salaries are possible
- Relocation specialist - Usually an executive position with the franchises – salaries are possible
- Syndicator - A person who uses a license to gain better access to investment properties and frequently takes a partnership position in those investments

CLERICAL AND SUPPORT

The real estate industry requires the support of a wide range of valuable helpers. You can find these positions with successful individual brokers, husband and wife teams, bigger teams, independent offices and franchise operations.

Receptionist

Every office has to have somebody who answers the phones and greets the public when they visit the office.

Office Administrator

This person is a coordinator and organizer. He or she sets up filing systems and processes paperwork and programs which are carried out for the benefit of the brokers and the company. Some examples include handling payroll, tax forms, bill paying, maintaining files for all the closed transactions, scheduling meetings and advertising.

Secretarial and Filing

In the more productive offices, there is so much detail work that the office administrator needs plenty of help. These people fill that needed role.

Personal Assistants

There are many successful agents who have enormous client lists and so many transactions they need a secretary-type person who works exclusively for them. This person gets to know the broker's clients and makes sure all the detail work is taken off the broker's plate so that the agent can concentrate on showing homes, making listing presentations, attending closings and other critical matters.

Team Assistants

There are numerous teams in the business. There are husband and wife teams, and some bigger teams where there is one primary broker who serves as the leader with as many as 15 team members who do the marketing, measuring, clerical work, filing and paperwork, delivering signs, making brochures, hosting open houses, writing ads, coordinating showings and all the other details. Usually, these larger teams process a whirlwind of activity.

To get these jobs, it is not enough to contact the receptionists of the various organizations. Most agents are independent contractors and the front desk in these offices does not always know of the openings which the individual agents have. Therefore, the prospective employee should ask if he or she can hang a brochure in the break-room offering to work for individual agents.

OTHER PROFESSIONALS

There are quite a few other associates who do not typically work within the walls of the real estate office itself but are critical to bringing real estate transactions to successful conclusions. Most of them experience peaks and valleys parallel to those of the agents. In most cases you would investigate these employment possibilities in their own offices, but some of the agents may be able to alert you of specific openings.

Corporate Positions

These are mostly "home-office" jobs consisting of both clerical and executive positions. Some of the executive jobs include things like relocation organizers, public relations, mass marketing, franchise promoters and others.

Escrow/Title Companies

Nearly every single transaction utilizes these people. They have clerical positions, researchers, office managers and transaction closers. The latter can work their way into some well-paying jobs.

Mortgage Brokers and Lenders

The main job of these professionals is to get loans approved for buyers. Their skill level varies widely. They try to get into the real estate offices to meet the brokers and offer their services. However, they have a high turnover rate and the agents don't want to be bombarded by them. Generally, once an agent finds a lender he likes, he becomes very loyal to that source. The better lenders can easily make a six-figure income, usually from commissions.

Home Inspectors

Friend or foe? These folks are usually self-employed and frequently aligned with larger franchise companies. During the normal residential transaction the buyer has a fair chance to have anybody he or she wants inspect the property. For those who lack expertise of their own or personal contacts who can do this for them, the home inspectors are trained to perform this service.

A lot of what they do is elementary but they do provide semi-expert inspection of the operating systems including plumbing, heating, electrical boxes, gas lines, and heating and air conditioning systems. Ordinarily, they are very thorough and the buyer who retains them ends up knowing more about the home than the seller knows.

The real value for these people comes in their communication skills. Naturally, the inspectors who make very good livings are the ones who don't inject unnecessary drama into the transactions. Their fee is usually several hundred dollars and some of them can get three inspections done in a single day, making for a very nice annual income.

Appraisers

Ordinarily when a buyer obtains a new loan, the lender requires an appraisal. These schooled professionals are very good at detail work. Since no home has an exact value they are usually inclined to think a home is worth whatever a buyer will pay for it. If they can find statistics to support the offered price there are not usually many hitches.

The fate of appraisers is a lot like that of home inspectors. Nobody expects them to compromise their integrity, but if they tend to look for ways to put deals together rather than ways to tear them apart, they are invited back into future transactions.

So, there you have it, a complete overview of the jobs in the industry. If you decide regular residential sales is not for you, Uncle Dave hopes you have discovered alternatives not previously considered. And, if you are a steady Eddie who knew what you wanted to do before reading this section and you still hold that same position, then you should have a good perspective on all of the important people who are devoted to helping you.

We talked about property management a little earlier, and I could write an entire book on that topic, but until then, perhaps this particular story will provide some insight into some of the issues in that branch of the business.

Uncle Dave's True Story #13: Evicting Children for Fun and Profit

I once rented out a three-bedroom, lower middle-class home to a family with four kids. Before we rented to them, we performed the same background check we did for anybody else. They checked out fine but none of that seemed to matter for long. The first month they paid their rent a couple of days late. After that, they got progressively later. Each month, we served the appropriate papers. Eventually, it was clear they were not going to catch up or move out on their own, so eviction was the only remaining alternative.

> *In Colorado, it takes nearly a month to complete the eviction process, but it takes longer in some other states.*

Usually, when we get to that point we can work with people

to reduce the drama for them, but all of our efforts were in vain with these people. We were not the only ones trying to work with them. Throughout the eviction process, there are several formal notices by the County Sheriff of the inevitable outcome, but these tenants disregarded all those warnings as well.

Two days before the scheduled eviction, the sheriff visited them to give them one final chance to move out on their own, but he met the same cavalier attitude they displayed throughout the process. They were not going to leave without a full measure of drama. It was late spring and afternoon rain showers were common.

I rounded up a bunch of boxes and plastic bags as well as a small crew of helpers. As expected, it was raining when we arrived at the property. The sheriff showed up a few minutes later. He went to the door to advise the tenants that he was there to oversee the procedure and to "keep the peace." But he was surprised to discover there were no adults in the home. Instead, he was greeted by seven kids, several of them under five years old. The rain was getting worse as he advised me of the situation and asked me what I wanted to do.

I wanted to reschedule the move-out, but that was not allowed. If you don't follow through when the sheriff is there, you have to start all over, which takes another month. That option was rejected. The procedure had to go on. I had another rental property on that block so I explained to the occupants of that home what happened and they agreed to keep an eye on the children until the parents showed up.

Other adults also took an interest in the matter. A couple of rain-soaked adults gathered to lend a hand to the children and my wife called the Social Services department to get assistance for the youngsters.

A couple of the youngest ones were crying as we hauled the furniture to the street and placed it by the road where the sheriff indicated. We tried to be respectful by covering up the belongings which might get damaged. An hour later, all their useful items were placed by the curb, but the parents were still invisible. It was time for the children to leave the home. The sheriff told them they had to step outside and off the property...which meant into the rain.

After the eviction, we drove by the property once each hour, to make sure the kids were safe. Some of them were playing in the street and others were huddled on the neighbor's porch. Eventually, the rain subsided. Finally, around 7:00 p.m., the parents arrived. We saw them laughing and joking around as they surveyed the matter and discussed the situation with their friends. By the next morning, they had successfully gathered most of their belongings and disappeared into oblivion.

In my own opinion, these people ought to be charged with child neglect. In spite of several formal notices advising them of their destiny, they could not be bothered to shelter their children from the ordeal. To compound their misdeeds, they were able to accumulate three additional children to subject to the situation. The parents of those children were equally elusive. These parents were so cavalier and irresponsible it defies description.

Think about it. What did you learn?

Hint: Consider the real victims in this story.

Go to page 223 for your Instant Experience.

Chapter 14 – PSSST! DID YOU HEAR ABOUT...?
or
Rogues and Misfits

I have spent a great deal of this book promoting the idea that most successful real estate professionals are normal everyday kinds of folks. This chapter is designed to prove that there are exceptions to every rule. Early on, I suggested I would share some gossipy stuff with you, so here is some juice for your amusement.

All of these stories are true. I personally know all these people. I have changed the names to protect the guilty... and me. You have probably met similar individuals.

Charlie B. Goode

Unlike his name, Charlie was not a very good boy. He started out as a superb young talent. He was a single fellow, handsome, and he had a delightfully contagious smile. No doubt, he caught the eye of all the eligible young women.

After attending a dynamic marketing seminar, Charlie returned to the office fired up and ready to slay all the dragons. He put together a marketing team and began to gather listings by the handful. After two months, Charlie had listings everywhere, and his early listings were closing at the rate of two to three per week. Our support staff was running frantic trying to keep up with all the detail work.

Then one Monday morning, an angry seller called our managing broker to announce Charlie had missed an appointment and was not returning calls. A short while later a similar call was received from a different client. The manager could not find our young dynamo anywhere. As it turned out, Charlie suddenly went out of town on the previous weekend. That would seem harmless enough, until the sheriff got involved.

A few months later, Charlie had a new roommate. They were destined to spend several years together. Apparently, all those listings and all that real estate activity were not exciting enough for this young man. As the story goes, Charlie was busted with a very large quantity of cocaine in the trunk of his luxury car and was rewarded with 48 months of free rent, behind bars.

I don't know what he is doing now. If he learned his lesson, he is still young enough and dynamic enough to achieve greatness. However, if he cannot live without vast quantities of drama, his dynamic personality is the stuff professional con men are made of. I hope he recovers. He was a nice fellow.

Tracie, the Trailblazer

All the successful female agents of today owe a great debt to Tracie and a few others like her. A generation ago, the real estate sales game was dominated by males. But Tracie was a misfit with enormous courage and she wanted to join the ranks.

Our heroine had been very successful in a previous sales job. She knew very little about real estate, but no old-school-stodgy-way-we've-always-done-it mentality was going to get in her way. With that extraordinary confidence she approached the sales manager in one of the top offices in the region. The male agents in that office dominated the market. They were turning out transactions by the dozens. Clearly, this was no place for beginners—especially a woman.

Even though no women had ever worked there before, her background earned her a trip through the door of the sales manager's office. Her happy-go-lucky personality was immediately contagious and the sales manager saw a lot of potential. But there were still two big problems. First, she had no significant real estate experience; second, the synergy of the office would be threatened if a woman, any woman, was to penetrate the network of good ol' boys.

The sales manager had a great idea. He set up three separate lunch appointments with Tracie and three of the most respected guys. Each fellow was to spend an hour with her and report back to the sales manager. That was a stroke of brilliance. Tracie was a bit of a looker but that bubbly personality of hers sealed the deal. All those studs thought she deserved a shot.

Naturally, there was a lot of resistance in the beginning, both with the gang at the office, and also with the public. But failure was not an option for this extra-special woman. All the obstacles just served to motivate her even more.

Her grit was immediately tested. Sexual harassment was not even a term in those days, so she was subjected to all the off-color, sexist jokes. She didn't complain to anyone; that would have been a mistake. Tracie knew exactly how to deal with those guys; she just laughed. The raunchier those jokes got, the more she laughed. They could not shake her.

Any of the normal learning mistakes she made were served up as examples of why women don't belong in the industry, but Tracie wouldn't quit. Naturally, when agents have that much fortitude, they have great potential. It did not take long before her business kicked in. All sorts of folks were being converted. Within a couple years, her sales numbers elevated her to the middle of the pack with some awesome months and occasional awards for being "salesman" of the month. There can be no doubt she had successfully become "one of the guys."

By the time I met Tracie, she had been in that office about six years. Several other women worked there by then. There was very little evidence of sexual bias anymore. Clearly, Tracie blew the doors wide open.

The sales manager learned from his technique too. I had to go to lunch with three of the agents before he would decide if I could fit in. One of my lunch appointments was with Tracie. She was like a pressure-release valve. She knew what it was like to seek a position in that office.

I owe Tracie a bit of gratitude for the way she treated me at my interview, but my debt amounts to small potatoes compared to what the masses of female agents owe her and others like her. Tracie was a pioneer who overcame enormous odds. Now, 60% of the membership of the National Association of Realtors is comprised of women. Tracie was a priceless gift to us all.

The Shark Twins

Randy and Richard are not biological twins but their shark-like style is identical. They love competition and will do anything or say anything to get that listing or sell that home. If Randy knows that the sellers are going to meet with several brokers, he tells the sellers he has a special deal for them and schedules his appointment so that he is "the last one in." That way he finds out what the seller liked about the other agents and then he claims to be better at that particular issue, regardless of what it is.

His high pressure sales tactics get him lots of business at the expense of weaker people. He has very little repeat business because people don't like his cut-throat ways, but that does not matter much because there are lots of vulnerable folks to be had.

Richard is just as bad. The rest of us see right and wrong in strict black-and-white terms, but he only sees varying shades of gray. As far as Richard is concerned when a customer says no, they really mean maybe and maybe means yes. Weak customers don't have a chance around either one of these two scoundrels. Their sellers pay top commissions and are pressured into selling their homes for less than necessary. Their buyers settle for properties they really don't want because they lack the ability to stand up to these fellows.

The Shark Brothers symbolize all the things the public hates about real estate agents. They are high-pressure, self-serving bad boys. They will gladly stretch the rules for another buck or two. They have no trouble lying to anybody just to get a deal closed. They don't care if they exploit other people as long as there are a few bucks to be pocketed. Their peers avoid them.

They get in trouble regularly. They are disciplined by their sales managers, the Association of Realtors, the Real Estate Commission and the legal system, but none of that discourages them.

Profits come first, second, third and everywhere else for the Sharks. Other people are merely prey to be devoured. And Randy and Richard are always hungry for more fresh meat.

JOKE TIME - Three competing brokers all had offices on the same side of one small street. One day one of the brokers put up a big new sign that said "We have the Best Brokers." Not to be outdone, the second broker put up an even bigger sign. It said, "We have the Best Listings." The third broker almost gave up, but then she had an idea. She put up the biggest sign of all. It said, "ENTER HERE."

Miss Sara Louise Proper Pants

Sara Louise is the kind of woman who would make her daddy proud. She always tries to do things the right way. She rarely makes waves. She is proper and professional in every way. Everybody respects Sara Louise.

She already had a worthy career before I met her. She was certainly successful and her image was very positive. She drove a flashy car and made a great first impression. She always wore nice clothes and just the right amount of makeup and jewelry.

She had good people skills, too. Her past clients were loyal to her and she had good systems in place to generate and serve new persons. Sara Louise was not especially a party animal but she liked to go to the social events.

She made her mistakes once in a while, but those were not because of anything sinister or irresponsible, until one particular convention. That was the weekend Miss Sara Louise took one giant step backwards—or should I say she "stumbled" one giant step backwards.

Unfortunately for our admired friend, one night she had way too much to drink, lost all control and tarnished a sparkling image. The embarrassing ordeal took place near the pool and you can guess what happened. We have probably all made similar mistakes, but this debacle was so out of character for her it left a lasting impression on those who know her.

Miss Proper Pants deserves to be forgiven for that one careless weekend because she has done so many things well, but I am certain that is one weekend she would love to do over.

Wasteful Willie

Willie is a worse money manager than the United States government. On the surface, that does not seem worthy of mention because we have all had financial problems from time to time. I admit that I have bounced a few checks in my lifetime. I have forgotten to put stamps on envelopes, which caused me to owe late fees to somebody. I have put the wrong check in the envelope. I have mailed out my bills planning on making a deposit to cover them and then failed to get the deposit made on time. I have made math errors in my check book ledger and then spent money I did not actually have. If there are other ways to screw up personal finances, Uncle Dave has probably done them too. I suspect the reader has had similar experiences. Our problems are a result of occasional human error and any damage from our shortcomings is negligible. But Wasteful Willie is different.

His financial indiscretions amount to disgraceful waste. I could give you several good examples, but I will stick with how he handles his income tax obligations. In case you do not know this, it is common for real estate agents to send the IRS quarterly payments because income tax dollars are not normally withheld from commission checks.

Willie makes an awesome income, normally well into the six-figure range. People who enjoy income like that have a large tax burden. Willie owes the IRS $20,000 or more per quarter but he never has the money to pay them. So, penalties and interest are added to the obligation and Willie has to make $25,000 or more in new commissions in the next month, just to catch up. And of course, there is a new tax obligation for the additional $25,000 he just made.

As I said earlier, it is the same story nearly every quarter. By the end of the year Willie pays more in penalties and interest charges than some people earn in that same year. Can you imagine the charitable work he could do with all that wasted money?

The obvious question is how can anybody consistently make that kind of income and always be broke? With a little better money management Willie could have guaranteed himself a fantastic retirement and used his wasted dollars for any number of worthwhile causes. Unfortunately, no such benefits will be enjoyed.

A lot of people struggle with finances. Some of them learn from their mistakes but others never do. Sadly, Willie is in the latter group. Naturally, it is nobody's business how Willie spends his money, but because of the lost opportunity to do something special with all those wasted dollars he qualifies as a tragic misfit.

The Blackjack Kid

His company had nearly 20 agents, about half of them specialized in selling rental properties to entry-level investors. In addition, there was a property management division with several hundred units to manage. The Kid had not yet reached his 30th birthday.

The kid owned the office building in which we worked, and there was a great conference room which contained a really cool table. There were a few occasions when a group of us would gather round that large table after work to play poker. It was a fun place.

Nobody enjoyed the friendly games more than the Kid. Naturally, the conversation rolled around to Las Vegas. Considering how much the Kid liked gambling it was a surprise to learn he had never been to the famous tourist trap. It should be no surprise that we scheduled a trip and several of us went there for a fun weekend.

Speaking for myself, one trip to Sin City each year is plenty, but the Kid enjoyed himself so much he wanted to go back and right away. A couple of us went along. Not long thereafter, he was looking for travel partners again, then again after that. Before long, everybody else was tired of visiting the town so the Kid went by himself many more times.

Then, one day a knock came at the door. Some of the investors of one of the apartment buildings which were managed by the Kid's company had some questions. A couple of them were former IRS agents so they knew how to investigate details. That was the beginning of the Kid's undoing. They demanded to see the books for their property. YIKES!

The next day, the Kid did not come to work, but the investor group did. You can guess what they discovered. Suffice it to say, they don't build all those fancy casinos by losing to people like the Kid. By the time it was over, we found out the Kid had a very big problem. We all knew he was going to the Entertainment Capital of the World way too often but we had no idea how much money he was betting, or more importantly, how much money he was losing—money that did not belong to him. By the time the dust settled, the losses were in the tens of thousands.

The Real Estate Commission has a fund to compensate people

who are damaged by the criminal activities of licensed brokers. The investors were awarded the maximum amount of $50,000 to cover some of their losses.

The real tragedy of this story was the Kid had phenomenal potential. He was enjoying an income stream in the quarter million a year range. FLUSH! He had his own group of investments. FLUSH! He had 20 licensed agents, all paying him a monthly income for working in his company. FLUSH! He was doing so well he was about to open a second office and compound his profits. FLUSH! All of those losses originated from a simple nickel-ante poker game in the back room, after work. What a shame.

So there you have the stories about some of the oddballs I have known. They serve to prove that normal agents fall victim to human frailties just like anybody else. My apologies to any of my colleagues who feel like they should have made my list, but this gang represents the first team. They may not be as interesting as the cast of *Saturday Night Live*, but they are certainly a very colorful group.

You have to admit that when it comes to reading books about real estate topics, these stories are a lot more entertaining than any of the "how-to" books.

It is a real bummer when good agents are denied success. Sometimes it is their own fault, as some of the previous characters proved, but it can also happen as a result of more innocent activities. The following story is a sad example of the misfortunes of a relatively innocent broker.

Uncle Dave's True Story #14: The Transactions That Did Not Happen

One day, a flier came across my desk wherein a local investor was liquidating 13 condos in a nearby complex. A quick phone call revealed that the listing agent was inexperienced but very nice. She told me that most of the units were rented out and the owner wanted to carry the loan (serve as the lender) for tax purposes. Both of those points appealed to me.

The asking price and interest rate were a little stiff, but I was willing to accept those minor issues. In the spirit of cooperation, I made a full-price offer. I agreed to all of the seller's proposed terms regarding down payment, interest rate and closing costs and everything else. A few days later I inspected the units and reaffirmed my cooperative nature by agreeing to accept the properties "as is."

At that point in the transaction, I had agreed to everything the seller could possibly want. He was not asked to make a single concession of any type. Things were going along fairly well when the young Realtor called to introduce a small problem. A few of the properties were actually owned in small partnerships so a whole new set of contracts needed to be executed and include the various sellers. Since I was the one with all the experience, I agreed to accommodate the situation and do all that paperwork.

I prepared a brand-new set of contracts, indicating the proper sellers and making each contract contingent on completing the acquisition of the other properties within the large group. The cumulative effect of the new contracts assured that we both got the same deal we previously accepted. Once again, the contracts contained everything he needed and wanted. I gave the new contracts to the listing Realtor and expected they would be signed without a hitch. But things were about to get very weird.

The listing agent called to announce she was on her way to my office with a counterproposal. When she arrived, she revealed that one of the properties had a minor title issue which would require a $25 fee to resolve. In spite of the fact that the matter was the owner's responsibility, he wanted me to pay the $25 for him, so he modified the relevant contract to indicate such. All that was needed was my initials to approve the entire transaction. But it was my turn to deliver a surprise.

> *His idea of sharing a sled is somebody else pulls it up the hill and he rides it back down.*

As far as I was concerned that was incredibly disrespectful. In all my years in the business, I had never seen a buyer more accommodating to a seller than I was toward him. I gave him everything he asked for. But he was not happy with 100%. He had to squeeze out just a little bit more. He wanted that extra $25. I told the nice lady Realtor the entire deal was off. I told her I was perfectly happy to keep the $25 and he could have his 13 condos back.

That may seem drastic but his actions convinced me I did not want to be involved in a long-term relationship with a person like that. I like to play "win/win," but it was clear that he liked to play "win all you can." His idea of sharing a sled is somebody else pulls it up the hill and he rides it back down.

Two months later I bought a 20-unit apartment building instead.

About one year later a fellow in my office, named Jim, posted ten new listings on the board in our break room. It was the same portfolio minus three properties, which the young Realtor eventually sold. In the end, it took the seller over two years to sell the final unit. He had to find 13 different buyers, negotiate with all of them, organize inspections, make concessions, spend advertising money, and attend 13 different closings. He was lucky Jim stuck with him through all of that.

Thereafter, the seller listed another 30 small properties with Jim—listings the first agent could have had. I don't know if the Realtor or the seller learned any lessons from this transaction, but what about you?

Think about it. What did you learn?

Hint: Consider the biggest loser in the story and the effect of a counter-proposal.

Go to page 224 for your Instant Experience.

Chapter 15 – YOUR INSTANT EXPERIENCE
or
Answers to Uncle Dave's True Stories

Uncle Dave's True Story #1 – The Three Stooges of Investing

Your Instant Experience: Some transactions offer great lessons from The Three-Legged Stool of Knowledge. This was one of those special cases. First, every buyer should know why they are buying a property and how they are going to get out of it. Typical home buyers may expect to live in a property for many years and decide they will cross that bridge when they get to it, but if buyers intend to live in a property for only a few years they should give consideration to this concept because stagnant or declining markets can hurt them financially. Our group never even considered an exit strategy and that was dangerous. As a result, we accepted the first offer that came along. To this day, Uncle Dave still does not know if we made a good deal or not.

Second, you can earn extra commissions by putting partnerships together. In this example, each one of us brought something to the relationship that the other two lacked. Similar situations come up in residential sales. If you meet somebody who lacks a key qualification to complete a transaction, do not give up without digging deeper. Parents can give their children money for a down payment to buy homes. Other family members can co-sign on loans for those with insufficient income.

Third, you do not have to restrict your thinking to residential transactions. There are plenty of opportunities for investors to pool their resources to enhance their buying power. The brokers who serve these people earn extra commissions and occasionally put some big-ticket transactions together (a lot more on that later). Assembling partnerships is a good way for you to pocket enough extra money to take Uncle Dave with you on your next vacation. How about a trip to Rome or salmon fishing in Alaska?

Uncle Dave's True Story #2 – The Cellar Dweller Feller

Your Instant Experience: Uncle Dave was fortunate to have such an interesting first transaction. My youthful enthusiasm was certainly rewarded. Here are some of the things I learned:

- Do not spend your commission dollars before you get them because lots of things can go wrong.
- Uncle Dave did not learn the value of past clients and mailing lists until five more years passed. As a result of that misfortune, I lost touch with early clients including this exemplary family who worked their way out of government housing.
- Working with first-time home buyers can be very fulfilling because a very modest home can be a castle to them.
- Non-conforming rooms have led to serious problems, so new regulations have been created to protect the public. Make certain you are familiar with fire and health codes to determine what is considered safe in your area. If somebody wants to use a room like that after you advise them of those codes, you should have them sign a statement acknowledging they are aware of the risks.

Uncle Dave's True Story #3 – Ungrateful to the Max

Your Instant Experience: In addition to pointing out how interesting the life of an independent contractor can be, there are two good lessons in this simple story. First, this transaction took place before professional home inspections became common. Along with the true story before it, where a boiler fell apart, this story illustrates why professional inspections are so useful. Sometimes you will have buyers who would like to save the few hundred dollars which the inspectors charge, but remember this: If something unexpected goes wrong with the home, many people look for somebody to blame. If you don't give them an alternative, they are probably going to blame you.

Second, you cannot please everyone. When something like this happens to you, don't dwell on it. If you complete enough transactions, it is bound to happen to you sooner or later. Just consider it to be an enigmatic symbol of your success.

Uncle Dave's True Story #4 – Enabled by the Disabled

Your Instant Experience: If you want to play with the big dogs, you cannot pee pee like a puppy. That is particularly true whenever you venture into commercial transactions. Those agents do not always belong to the Association of Realtors, so they play by a different set of rules than the residential brokers. It is your job to know those rules before you get involved in specific transactions. Uncle Dave should have registered his customer with the listing broker before giving away the marketing brochure.

Second, it would have been easy for Uncle Dave to get irritated with his contact, but self-control, good people skills and a positive attitude served to recapture all the losses and a whole lot more. Real estate is like many other professions. If you are not sincerely motivated to overcome the type of problems mentioned in this story you might as well look for another job.

Uncle Dave's True Story #5 - Beneath the Sister's Habit

Your Instant Experience: There are several good lessons in this story: First, the benefit of a sphere of influence cannot be overstated. In this case Uncle Dave had a shot at Margie's business even though I was woefully less qualified than the other fellow.

Second, whenever somebody wants to sell their existing home and buy another one, the best procedure is to sell the current home first. To avoid an ugly situation, the seller and broker insert a provision in the listing agreement, and the eventual contract, which states the owner does not have to close the transaction or move until such time as they locate a suitable replacement property.

Third, do not assume that people realize how important their business is to you. It is your duty to explain it to them and not their job to figure it out. Nearly every new agent becomes a victim to similar circumstances. We don't want to be pushy so we work hard for somebody, believing that they will appreciate our loyalty and wholeheartedly return the sentiment. The problem is we assume too much. One newcomer told me that a buyer she was working with actually told her, "You have done so much for us already, we didn't want to bother you again, so we just called the guy whose name was on the sign and made him do all the work." It does not get any clearer than that.

In this story, Margie made it perfectly clear that she was in touch with another agent, but I did nothing to deserve her loyalty. She simply went with the first person to find what she wanted. That makes perfect sense.

To avoid getting in that same jam, Uncle Dave suggests you offer to trade loyalty with your customers. Tell them you will help them get the best possible deal and protect them from the pitfalls many buyers make if they will agree to work exclusively with you. Most of them are pleased to discover you actually know how to make sense out of all that scary paperwork.

Hopefully, you can learn this lesson now and avoid the inevitable pain the rest of us endured.

Uncle Dave's True Story #6 – Crooked Profits

Your Instant Experience: The new licensee can benefit by understanding several key points within this true story. As stated in this chapter many agents have oddball traits, and nobody ever called Uncle Dave normal, but Bob and I made nearly one million dollars each because of transactions like this. Working with investors is cool.

> ### *You will always have somebody to work with...*

Second, if you have good investors among your client base, you will always have somebody to work with because investors are always willing to make a profit. Whenever typical residential transactions seem scarce, go find a good deal somewhere; then, find someone who would like to make a profit. There are lots of them. So, go get them.

Third, the lady agent who walked in and ran away quickly while Bob and I were inspecting the home offered a quintessential example of an agent blinded by individual biases. Some agents won't show defective homes or low-priced properties because they see low commissions or extra headaches. In this situation Uncle Dave recognized profit dollars in addition to commission dollars. By the time Johnnie paid me off, I received two commission checks and a nice profit. Being creative really paid off.

Fourth, single people who are willing to move around a lot can be great allies. You can earn extra commissions and they can earn profits by teaming up. Sometimes, you can join them in a share of the profits by forming partnerships. Practically anybody who is not sensitive to school issues is a good candidate. Ask people if they have too much money. Most of them will laugh and say no. Follow up, and find out if they would like to employ this technique with you. Four or five such clients can fill any holes in your income stream.

Fifth, every home has some value. In this case, the income stream made the home worth more than Bob paid for it, but we were the only ones who recognized the opportunity. While others were focused on bricks with cracks, Bob and Uncle Dave observed a monthly pot of gold at the end of a low-cost rainbow.

WHEW! That transaction offered us a lot of "experience."

Uncle Dave's True Story #7 – I Do, I Do, and I Do, Too

Your Instant Experience: This transaction confirms the information discussed earlier in this chapter. Namely, take care of your past clients. They are an excellent source of repeat business.

My son suggested, each time you attend a closing be sure to give your clients a business card of a good divorce attorney.

Uncle Dave's True Story #8 – In the Eye of the Beholder

Your Instant Experience: The Fair Housing Laws require brokers to make "reasonable allowances" whenever we work with disabled people. By my expressing my concern with Louie and bringing his own friend into the transaction, he knew I wanted the best for him.

That attitude netted me brownie points with the referring client plus two nice commission checks from Louie. Always put your people first, and the profits will follow.

Uncle Dave's True Story #9 – A Million from Trash

Your Instant Experience: None of those fantastic profits could have been gained were it not for Uncle Dave's long-term commitment to the concepts of Hate Debt, Save Consistently and Invest Wisely.

This transaction also reveals an interesting but unnatural negotiation technique. There are occasions when the best tactic is to recognize a good opportunity and seize it before it gets away. In this case, I had an inside track to a great deal. If I would have made a lower offer for these properties it might have taken several days to come to an agreement. In that time the other agents in the listing office might have learned about the properties and a bidding war may have ensued.

Uncle Dave has observed plenty of disappointed residential buyers and agents because they opened the door for competitors. There are occasions when we should not take that risk. This was one of those times. How much difference would it have made if I saved a few thousand dollars by shrewd negotiating? On the other hand, how much difference would it have made if I was outbid and missed out on the deal altogether?

The better agents instinctively know when their buyers are exposed to similar circumstances. Those who can properly identify the situation and advise their buyers effectively go to the closing table and begin working on their next transaction. But the agents who are oblivious to the situation allow opportunities for disappointment and cannot get to their next deal. Now you should be able to join the former group.

Another point is worth mentioning. If you become an investor and you find yourself competing for a worthwhile property, sometimes it is smart to let the listing agent keep the full commission. That small concession can determine who gets the property. As you would guess, Stan continues to call me with his new listings.

Uncle Dave's True Story #10 – The Parlay of 49th Avenue

Your Instant Experience: I don't know what Larry did with his $500 but my colleague is among a gigantic group of fine agents who rarely take full advantage of the fantastic opportunities that are available in their very own offices, and sometimes right on their own desks. Commissions are nice but they come and go. However, proper investments can pay you passive income month after month for the rest of your life.

Larry made $500 or so off of that property. Bob made about $15,000 before he sold out. I made $37,000 in profit, which became half of a down payment on a 23-unit apartment building that I still own. That apartment building has risen in value by $600,000 over the past decade.

Bob is a quintessential example of a Fat Cat investor who can make you wealthy, provided you are willing to find good deals and share them. You can make more money off of the Bobs in the world than you can by investing your own money. Those Bobs need you and you need them. You each bring something to the deal that the other person lacks. Go find a few Bobs.

Finally, when Clark the lender saw how good the deal was, he wanted in on similar ones. Clark knew lots of people and other potential investors whom Uncle Dave could have met, but I already had plenty of investors, so I turned him down. However, Clark's request illustrates what happens to brokers who take this kind of business seriously: namely, investors come to you.

Uncle Dave's True Story #11 – King Poop and Peaches

Your Instant Experience: This is a classic example of inside information obtained in an office that was well matched to me. Kathy and I put that deal together before anybody else ever heard about it. However, I hope you also realized that Kathy should have bought this home herself.

Contrary to the true story of an earlier chapter, where a blind man named Louie could "see" exactly which property was best for him, the trained professionals in this story were blind to the obvious. And, their "vision" was not their only defective sense. When those agents visited this home, they also allowed their own noses to betray them. They were so concerned with the stinky problems and insignificant commissions that they missed the pleasing aroma of cash flow and handsome profits. When it comes to the agents in this transaction, it is their perspective that really stinks.

Anybody who has ever changed a diaper or visited an outhouse or worked on sewer pipes would gladly perform those tasks for a couple hours in exchange for $140,000.

Uncle Dave's True Story #12 – The Smoke House

Your Instant Experience: This transaction reveals why building a positive image is so important. This woman was fortunate that Keith entered her life. This extraordinary man has a reputation of kindness and decency that he has established over many years. That was why somebody introduced him to this tragic woman. He helped turn everything around for her. He replaced the symbol of a sad life with a new hope. He may have even saved her life, and I know that was a lot more important to him than any paycheck.

Keith has spent his entire career acting like this. He has shown us all that real estate is about a lot more than bricks and transactions. It is about people.

Uncle Dave's True Story #13 – Evicting Children for Fun and Profit

Your Instant Experience: This story is relevant because we have discussed property management as a career option and I have spent a fair amount of time trying to encourage readers to acquire investment properties. If you do either of those things, you will find yourself in some vulnerable situations such as this one. Properly handling situations like this will enhance your long-term success. Here is what you need to absorb from this story:

Some members of the public consider landlords to be greedy and insensitive. They suppose these evil rent-collectors are essentially willing to evict children for fun and profit. I suspect there will be those who read this story and conclude that I should have shown more compassion and rescheduled the eviction, even if it took another month. But there was no guarantee that similar frustrations would be absent the next time around. The evicted parents never showed a hint of responsibility toward the matter. The landlord was not the problem.

If someone burgles a home to steal furniture that they need, they would be subject to arrest. We do not expect the victimized family to get by without their furniture while some thief enjoys it.

If people are hungry and steal a side of beef they can go to jail. We do not ask the butcher to forfeit a month's food.

If parents grab hundreds of dollars' worth of clothes off the shelves in a store and jump in an awaiting get-away car, they are engaging in criminal activities. We would not ask the retail store to turn the other cheek whenever criminals confiscate their goods in trade. In all of these cases, it is easy to see who is misbehaving and who the victim of the misbehavior is.

Landlords are no different. We sell space between walls. We cannot afford to give away the only product we have. We have bills just like all these other business people.

We do not want to evict people, but sometimes they leave us no choice. By the time we get our property back to the market, we have absorbed substantial expenses including rent losses, cleanup and maintenance costs, advertising, ongoing utilities, taxes, insurance, interest payments on our loans, and a great deal of time. It is wholly appropriate for a landlord to protect against such losses.

Compassion is a wonderful quality, but you are not responsible for the shortcomings of others. If you find yourself in a situation like this, do all you can to protect the innocent, but you do not need to absorb excessive losses. Your family is innocent, too.

Uncle Dave's True Story #14 – Deal... or no Deal?

Your Instant Experience: This is one of my favorite stories because of the irony. Namely, a powerful lesson can be learned from a true story about 13 transactions which never did happen.

The chapter that preceded this story was about misfits and

unfortunately the Realtor in this story ends up being one of those. Sadly she is "The Biggest Loser" because everybody else came out okay: (a) I bought another property; (b) The seller eventually sold his entire portfolio of unwanted inventory; and (c) Jim picked up a very nice package of listings. On the other hand, the Realtor under discussion had thirteen commission checks in her hand and lost all but three of them, and she had to do a lot of extra work with other people to get those transactions completed. After that, she lost all the other commissions that Jim got instead of her. Her total loss: 40 commission checks!

Uncle Dave derives no pleasure from the Realtor's misfortune. She was simply the victim of her own inexperience and a greedy seller. It is most unfortunate she did not fully understand that brokers must "represent" their client's interests, and part of that obligation is to be certain the clients know the potential consequences of their choices.

The Realtor should have told her client that a counter proposal equals a rejection of a contract. Most professional agents would have been able to explain the risk better or at least offer to pay the $25 themselves. True professionals know to get the signature NOW! Her innocent failure to accomplish that objective revealed a side of the seller which was not previously known: namely, that he exploited people whenever he could. That killed the deal because Uncle Dave did not want to be involved with somebody like that.

EGRESS

Most endings are followed by new beginnings, and after 68,000 words we have arrived at that point. My objective was to show you how to survive beyond a precarious beginning. You also needed to know how to use the business to enhance your lifestyle and eventually provide you with a comfortable retirement by becoming your own best client. And finally, I wanted you to understand the importance of "giving back." I hope you believe we have accomplished all of that.

The things we discussed are not mere theories. They are the choices and practices of real brokers, and now you have met them. If all of this seems a little overwhelming to you, I would like to remind you one final time of my troubled past. I am not special in any way and I have enjoyed a fabulous career. The other brokers I have introduced you to are not extraordinary people either. Most of us are a lot like you. That is why there is room for you in our business. Just be certain you actively pursue the things we talked about, rather than wait for the universe to bring success to you on a silver platter – because it will not.

Now I have completed this circle, but you have just gotten started. Regardless of whether you have decided to proceed full speed ahead or slam on the brakes or take a sharp turn onto some side street, you should have a strong foundation for your decision.

I hope you have enjoyed the real life stories at the end of each chapter and the "Uncle Dave" approach as worthy alternatives to the format of typical nonfiction books. My goal was to provide useful information that is not usually found in other real estate books and deliver it in a more entertaining way. If I have succeeded in that regard please consider it my pleasure to have been allowed inside your mind for this time we have shared.

Finally, local laws and customs can vary and each person's situation is unique. Before you act on any of the ideas contained in this book, remember to confirm with your own experts exactly how any legal, tax or marketing matters will affect you personally.

Feel free to let me know what you think. Uncle Dave hopes to visit with you again, soon.

Thanks for reading
Instant Experience for Real Estate Agents.

Uncle Dave

> **WARNING: Do not copy the following document. It is for informational purposes only. You should consult your own attorney to develop a version that applies to you.**

Appendix One – Partnership Agreement
SAMPLE PARTNERSHIP AGREEMENT

WHEREAS, Uncle Dave (hereafter "Manager") and Fat Cat (hereafter "Investor") desire to enter into a Partnership Agreement,

WHEREAS, Manager and Investor agree to purchase certain real property (hereafter "Property") to wit:
CONDO UNIT 1234 (legal description)
Also known as 1137 Heavenly Avenue, city and state, zip.

WHEREAS, Investor pays the initial down payment and Manager provides management services for a period of five (5) years, beginning February 35, 2020 (hereafter "the management period").

NOW, THEREFORE, in consideration of the mutual covenants herein contained, it is agreed that:

1. Prior to the expiration of the Management Period, the Manager shall be responsible for the daily management of the Property but will not be compensated therefor.
2. At the end of the management period, the daily management obligations will be shared equally by the Manager and the Investor.
3. Investor shall provide initial down payment and obtain the loan to acquire the Property.
4. Following the acquisition and closing for the Property, the following documents shall be executed:
    a. Investor shall sign a Quit Claim Deed to Managing

Partner and Investor, effectively transferring one-half undivided interest in all rights, title and interest that Investor acquired as a result of said closing: and,

    b.   Manager shall execute an Indemnification Statement to effectively take responsibility for one-half of the original amount of the loan as acquired by the Investor and which is secured by the Property described herein.

5.   Following the expiration of the Management Period, the Investor shall not have down payment reimbursed; however, in the event the property is sold prior to the expiration of the Management Period, the Investor will receive a partial refund of her down payment as follows:

    a.   If the resale closing date is after one (1) year following the original acquisition date but before two and one-half (2 ½) years following the original acquisition date, Investor shall be entitled to one-half of her original down payment, or,

    b.   If the resale closing date is after two and one-half (2 ½) years following the original acquisition date but before four (4) years following the original acquisition date, Investor shall be entitled to one-quarter of her original down payment.

6.   All profits, losses, closing costs, income and expenses shall be borne equally by the Manager and the Investor.

7.   In the event either party desires to terminate this agreement or in the event of death or disability of either party, the surviving party shall have certain rights and options as follows:

DEATH, DISABILITY OR VOLUNTARY DEPARTURE BY MANAGER

In the event the Manager dies or becomes disabled and therefore is incapable of carrying out the obligations herein, his estate shall secure the services of a professional property manager. Said estate shall pay all costs for said property manager's services until the Management Period has expired.

In the event the Manager desires to terminate his obligations herein, he may do so prior to the expiration of the Management Period, provided he does the following:

1. Secures written permission from the Investor; and,
2. Forfeits all rights, title and interest in the Property to the Investor; and,
3. Is not compensated for any efforts he or she expended in the management of the Property.

Following the expiration of the Management Period, the Manager may terminate this agreement, provided he does the following:

1. Provide written notice to the Investor of his "intent to terminate the partnership." The Investor shall then have the option to buy out the Manager for ten thousand dollars (or 40% of the equity or...). The Investor shall have 45 days from receipt of said notice to tender payment to the Manager or this option shall be waived; however,
2. If the Investor does not elect to exercise the preceding option, the Manager shall be entitled to secure offers for his interest in the property on any terms he deems acceptable. In the event the Manager secures an acceptable offer, he shall tender a copy to the Investor and the Investor shall have five (5) business days to notify the Manager in writing of the "Investor's election to match the offer." Said notification shall be binding on the Investor. If subsequently the Investor is unable or unwilling to in fact match the offer and perform according to the terms contained in the offer, the Investor shall have automatically waived any additional options to match any other offers received thereafter by the Manager. Failure of the Investor to notify the Manager within the aforesaid five (5) business days shall constitute a

waiver by the Investor of any further options to match said offer or any offers received thereafter by the Manager.

DEATH, DISABILITY OR VOLUNTARY DEPARTURE BY INVESTOR

In the event the Investor dies or becomes disabled and therefore is incapable of carrying out the obligations herein, her estate shall be bound by the terms of this Agreement.

In the event the Investor desires to terminate her obligations herein, she may do so prior to the expiration of the Management Period, provided she does the following:

1. Secures written approval from the Manager; and,
2. Forfeits all of rights, title and interest in and to the Property to the Manager; and,
3. Is not compensated for any monies expended for the acquisition or ownership of the Property.

Following the expiration of the Management Period, the Investor may elect to terminate this agreement, provided she does the following:

1. Provide written notice to the Manager of her "intent to terminate the partnership." The Manager shall then have the option to buy out the Investor for $6,000 (or 29% of the equity, or...) in cash or certified funds. The Manager shall have 45 days from receipt of said notice to tender payment to the Investor or this option shall be waived; however,
2. If the Manager does not elect to exercise the preceding option, the Investor shall be entitled to secure offers for her interest in the Property on any terms she deems acceptable. In the event the Investor secures an acceptable offer, she shall tender a copy to the Manager and the Manager shall have five (five) business days to notify the Investor in writing of

the "Manager's election to match the offer." Said notification shall be binding on the Manager. If subsequently the Manager is unable or unwilling to in fact match the offer, the Manager shall have automatically waived any additional options to match any other offers received thereafter by the Investor. Failure of the Manager to notify the Investor within the aforesaid five (5) business days shall constitute a waiver by the Manager of any further options to match said offer or any other offers received thereafter by the Investor.

In the event either party herein brings suit to enforce the terms of this Agreement, the prevailing party may be awarded reasonable attorney's fees.

This agreement shall be binding upon and inure to the benefit of the heirs and successors of the respective parties.

_____
Uncle Dave, date

_____
Linda the Investor, date

Notary stuff

> **WARNING: Do not copy the following document. It is for informational purposes only. You should consult your own attorney to develop a version that applies to you.**

Appendix Two-Assignment

SAMPLE ASSIGNMENT AGREEMENT

This Assignment Agreement (hereafter "Agreement") is entered into this ____ day of _____, 2020, by and between Uncle Dave and Linda the Investor, collectively referred to as the Parties.

WHEREAS, on _____, 2020 Uncle Dave entered into a contract to buy that certain property (hereafter "Property") to wit:

CONDO UNIT 1234 (legal description)
Also known as 1137 Heavenly Avenue, city and state, zip,

WHEREAS, the Parties are entering into this Agreement to identify the terms and conditions to which they have agreed regarding the transfer of all rights title and interest in the contract and the Property from Uncle Dave to Linda the Investor,

NOW, THEREFORE, in consideration of the foregoing and the mutual promises set forth below, the Parties agree as follows:

1. Uncle Dave hereby assigns all of his rights, title and interest in the contract and the property to Linda the Investor.
2. Linda the Investor has reviewed the contract and agrees to its terms and conditions.
3. Both Parties acknowledge that they have entered into a separate Partnership Agreement dated _____ in which they have identified other terms and conditions to which they have agreed regarding the Property and their ongoing relationship.

Uncle Dave, date
_____

Linda the Investor, date
Notary stuff

Other books by this author

Stop Flushing Your Money Down the Drain

ISBN 978-1-937862-63-3

Contact the author at Dave@UncleDave'sRealEstate.com

Copies of this author's books may be ordered from
www.bookcrafters.net
and other online bookstores

This book available in digital format.